W9-AKC-846

Literacy and Bilingualism

James D. Williams
University of North Carolina, Chapel Hill

and

Grace Capizzi Snipper
Los Angeles Unified School District

Longman
New York & London

Literacy and Bilingualism

Copyright © 1990 by Longman.
All rights reserved.
No part of this publication may be reproduced,
stored in a retrieval system, or transmitted
in any form or by any means, electronic, mechanical,
photocopying, recording, or otherwise,
without the prior permission of the publisher.

Longman, 95 Church Street, White Plains, N.Y. 10601

Associated companies:
Longman Group Ltd., London
Longman Cheshire Pty., Melbourne
Longman Paul Pty., Auckland
Copp Clark Pitman, Toronto

Executive editor: Naomi Silverman
Production editor: Inkwell Publishing Services
Production coordinator: Ann P. Kearns
Cover design: Thomas Slomka, THOMAS WILLIAM DESIGN
Text art: Fineline, Inc.
Production supervisor: Priscilla Taguer

Library of Congress Cataloging-in-Publication Data

Williams, James D. (James Dale), 1949–
    Literacy and bilingualism / James D. Williams and Grace Capizzi
Snipper.
        p. cm.
    Includes bibliographical references.
    ISBN 0-8013-0195-5
    1. Education, Bilingual—United States. 2. English language—
Study and teaching—United States—Foreign speakers. 3. Literacy—
United States. I. Snipper, Grace Capizzi. II. Title.
LC3731.W54 1990
371.97′00973—dc20   89-12987
                                                         CIP

ABCDEFGHIJ-HA-99 98 97 96 95 94 93 92 91 90

I would like to dedicate this book to my wife, Ashley, and to my son, Austin.

—JDW

I would like to dedicate this book to my husband, Steve.

—GCS

Contents

CHAPTER 3

CHAPTER 4

CHAPTER 5

CHAPTER 6

CHAPTER 7

CHAPTER 8

CHAPTER 9

Preface

This book identifies and analyzes the mechanisms and issues in literacy—reading and writing—as they relate to bilingualism. It synthesizes a wide range of current theories and research and then makes concrete suggestions on how to develop literacy skills among students in bilingual classrooms. It provides credential candidates, teachers, and students of language with the background necessary to meet the educational needs of nonnative English-speaking students. It also dispels many of the misconceptions that often surround bilingualism and is designed to give readers the resources to become more effective instructors.

The text developed out of our respective work in literacy and bilingualism. Our backgrounds—Jim's in rhetoric and psycholinguistics and Grace's in sociolinguistics and language planning—stem from different philosophical outlooks that, when aligned, serve to provide more depth and breadth to this text. As an operational assumption, we take the position that there are psychological and linguistic universals that characterize language and that they are related to sociological factors that influence language use. Thus our approach is fundamentally psychosocial. We see language as a social action that shapes individuals as well as the societies in which they live. In this view, an interactive process exists that, as language is used to accomplish specific tasks, defines both the self and the community.

The book consists of nine chapters. The first chapter defines literacy along three dimensions governed by context and social expectations. It describes the characteristics of functional literacy, cultural and academic literacy, and critical literacy, laying the groundwork for much of what follows in later chapters. The second chapter addresses current and traditional models of reading and writing. It provides a detailed analysis of the mechanisms related to processing texts and then discusses some of the ways in which reading and writing are related.

Chapter 3 defines bilingualism, examining language proficiency, first-and second-language acquisition, and the relationship between proficiency and literacy. In addition, it describes the concept of language transfer and the role transfer plays in developing literacy skills among bilingual students. It concludes with an analysis of the social context of bilingualism.

Chapter 4 focuses on educational programs that use more than one language for instruction. It discusses the assumptions and goals of the major types of programs, exploring some of the philosophical and political issues that influence how they are structured. Programs are grouped into three categories: bilingual education programs, language immersion programs, and other language programs that include foreign-language classes for mainstream English speakers and private tutorials designed to preserve the language and culture of ethnolinguistic minorities.

Chapter 5 begins with an analysis of bilingualism and intelligence, summarizing a range of studies that present conflicting data on the intellectual abilities of bilinguals. It continues with a discussion of cognitive development to provide a framework for what we do in the classroom. The question of the relationship between mind and language is explored in detail, with particular attention given to the idea that language and literacy influence cognition. The chapter concludes with a framework for teaching strategies aiming at biliteracy. This framework consists of three student categories—preliterate, literate, and postliterate—that we use to propose specific pedagogical techniques.

Chapter 6 focuses on a range of topics related to teaching English in a meaningful context. It begins with an analysis of the various methods currently available for teaching a second language. It analyzes the more prominent approaches, noting their strengths and weaknesses. The chapter outlines an approach that provides a "whole-language," literature-based methodology for teaching literacy and language. The remainder of the chapter is devoted to examining some of the ways this approach can be used with preliterate, literate, and postliterate students.

Chapter 7 deals specifically with reading instruction. It pays special attention to the reclassification of students who began in bilingual programs as limited English proficient (LEP) and learned to read in the native language with the intention of shifting to an English-only program. Consistent with the discussion of literacy in Chapters 1 and 2, Chapter 7 reviews three theoretically sound approaches used to teach reading: the language experience approach (LEA), the core literature approach, and the reading-while-listening approach. The chapter examines in detail how they can be used to develop literacy in a bilingual context.

Chapter 8, focusing on students who have been reclassified as English proficient, offers a detailed analysis of how to develop a classroom environment that takes advantage of the benefits inherent in interactive learning. It describes a

CHAPTER 1

What Is Literacy?

OVERVIEW

This chapter begins by stressing the social nature of literacy, noting that to be literate has meant different things during different historical periods. In addition, to be literate means different things in different situations or, as they are called, "social contexts." It is therefore possible to be literate in one context but not in another. For example, a middle school student reading and writing at the seventh-grade level could be deemed literate among her peers but illiterate among university graduate students.

To help clarify such distinctions, three broad categories of literacy are generally associated with social contexts. Educators recognize *functional, cultural*, and *critical* literacy. Functional literacy is often related to basic writing (coding) and reading (decoding) skills that allow people to produce and understand simple texts. Cultural literacy emphasizes the need for shared experiences and points of reference to fully comprehend texts. And critical literacy is related to identifying the political component inherent in reading and writing.

PERSPECTIVES ON LITERACY

Today ideas about literacy are more complicated than they were three or four decades ago, because literacy has become more overtly politicized. For years the ability to read and write well was seen simply as part of being educated, which in turn was associated with income. Few students over the last four decades, for example, have escaped a lecture on the difference between what a high school graduate earns compared to what a college graduate earns. Recently, however, growing numbers of people have come to recognize that the ability to read and write well is linked to more than salary. It is often a key factor not only in the degree of self-determination people have but also in the amount of influence and power they can exert to shape the character and direction of their communities (see Apple, 1982; Freire & Macedo, 1987; Graff, 1987).

Admittedly, the complex nature of literacy makes it difficult to define. It is shaped by historical and social factors that vary from one period to another and from one "discourse community" to another. This latter term is usually understood as the common ground established through shared experiences, values, and language (which immediately suggests potential difficulties for nonnative English-speaking students in our schools).

We gain a clearer understanding of how the concept of literacy can change if we consider, for example, that in eighteenth-century America simply being able to sign one's name was considered evidence of literacy. The young nation's agrarian economy made few demands on people for reading and writing skill. Most information was transmitted orally, so there was little need for high-level literacy skills. If someone needed to send a letter but didn't know how to write, it was possible to hire a scribe who could.

Our society is now far more complex and, despite dire predictions from a few prognosticators who claim that videos are causing the end of the written word, the need for reading and writing skill is greater than it's ever been. On a pragmatic level, the chief executives of the nation's top businesses don't hesitate to point out that they need new employees who can read and write far more than they need people who can operate computers. To address that need, large numbers of corporations hire consultants to teach their employees the literacy skills they must have to perform successfully on the job. For example, major accounting firms like Peat, Marwick, Mitchell, and Coopers and Lybrand routinely send their new accountants to a series of classes designed to help them become better readers and writers. And of course, all of these accountants are recent college graduates.

Clearly, none of us is likely to accept a signature as a demonstration of literacy, but as the example just mentioned suggests, we quickly get to a point where we recognize that literacy is not a uniform concept. People deemed literate in one context may be deemed illiterate in another. You may be very adept at reading and understanding your college textbooks, but you may find it impossible to read and understand a legal contract or a financial statement. In these contexts you may be essentially illiterate.

Over the last several years, scholars have been working to formulate more inclusive definitions of literacy. The popular view of literacy as being simply the ability to read and write is insufficient when investigations of language are exploring the role texts play in defining individuals and the communities they live in, exploring the role texts play in shaping gender relationships and class structure, exploring the role language plays in personal development and empowerment. One result of such work is that three broad categories have come to be widely used to describe a range of behaviors associated with what it means to be literate today: *functional literacy, cultural literacy*, and *critical literacy* (McLaren, 1988).

The focus of literacy research and theory has been significantly influenced by a search for community (or communities) and by efforts to explore what it means to share knowledge, experiences, and values (see Bender, 1982; Habermas, 1962; Kiechel, 1989; Naisbitt, 1982). We have no way of knowing for certain what factors are driving this shift in emphasis, although some writers see it as a response to the breakdown of traditional support networks caused by mobility and urbanization. We can only observe marked efforts on a number of institutional levels to move away from individualistic, hierarchical patterns of behavior to collaborative ones.

The resulting influence on instruction has been significant. We will address the specific pedagogical issues in later chapters, but by way of preface we would note that emphasizing collaboration has already started to change the way writing is taught in this country, and there are indications that it is also changing the way reading is taught. The focus on writing as a process and the move in many districts away from basal readers to a Big Book program or a Learning Experience Approach are two reflections of this change. We will argue throughout this book that modifying what we may think of as the traditional approach to reading and writing instruction can have a profound effect on the literacy of our nonnative English-speaking students.

We recognize, however, that the hurdle presented by school discourse is made more difficult for these students by the existence of conflicting positions on the very nature of literacy. Education (and thus reading and writing instruction) is usually considered a social science, yet academic literacy is usually considered a humanistic enterprise.

As Patricia Bizzell (1988) points out, the social sciences view literacy as effecting a *behavioral* change in individuals that influences how they see and understand the world. Reading, for example, allows people to sample vicariously the experiences and perspectives of others and to compare them with their own. We like to think the result is less provincialism and greater tolerance for diversity. Humanists, on the other hand, "tend to dichotomize nonliterate and literate states of being, and to reify the two states into all-embracing conceptual universes . . ." (p. 142). They argue that literacy alters the quality of the mind itself, changing how people see the world by fundamentally modifying the way they think, giving them the ability to reason abstractly.

The humanist view of literacy is strongly advocated by writers such as Olson (1977) and Ong (1982), who claim that abstract thinking is impossible in the absence of reading and writing ability. It proposes that language—specifically, written language in alphabetic form—influences and develops thought. Although social scientists generally consider this notion extremely simplistic, if not simply incorrect, it has nevertheless been used repeatedly to help justify monolingual immersion programs and to support the claim that mastering Standard English has cognitive consequences.

In the face of research in the social sciences that has repeatedly repudiated the idea that literacy has measurable effects on cognition (Scribner & Cole, 1981), a topic we examine in detail in Chapter 5, the humanist view has recently been revised; currently we find much discussion of the connection between "critical thinking skills" and reading and writing ability. The terms have changed, but the pedagogical implications have not.

DEFINING LITERACY

Implicit in our discussion so far is the suggestion that any attempt to define literacy must take into account the contexts in which reading and writing occur. A viable definition must be rhetorical in that it addresses questions that go beyond skill level to aim, purpose, audience, and text. With these factors as guides, the sections that follow trace the distinctions that exist among the three types of literacy mentioned above.

Functional Literacy

In the past, literacy was generally used to describe simply the ability to read and write, with an emphasis on reading. Now *functional literacy* is often used to denote the ability to read and write well enough to understand signs, read newspaper headlines, fill out job applications, make shopping lists, and write checks. The nation's numerous campaigns against illiteracy are concerned primarily with these fundamental skills, and we often hear that between 40 and 60 million American adults are functionally illiterate (see Kozol, 1985).

If functional literacy is reading and writing at some minimal level, just what *is* that level? Answering this question is not easy because it's difficult to specify the behaviors that define minimal skills. Where writing is concerned, the references to filling out job applications are not particularly informative.

The problem regarding writing is twofold. First, no one has yet described writing skill in a way that has any valid correspondence to age or grade level. Kellogg Hunt's (1965) important research confirmed the existence of a developmental component in writing performance: As children grow older, they produce longer sentences through longer clause structures. But his work did not attempt to establish norms for sentence length and grade level in the way that reading researchers have. Second, it is not easy to determine to what extent an illiterate person's difficulties with writing are influenced by the inability to read. For example, people who cannot read job applications to begin with would not know what written responses to make; people who don't know how to fill out a check well enough for it to be cashed probably would not find themselves in a position to open a checking account, and so on.

Initially, setting a minimal level for reading skill appears far simpler because we have a range of reading tests that allow us to convert raw scores into grade-level equivalents. Many of these tests, however, were normed during the 1960s, so it's often difficult to interpret exactly what a particular reading score means. At the University of North Carolina in Chapel Hill, for example, many of the entering freshmen, all of whom take the Nelson-Denny Reading Test, have reading levels between the eighth and tenth grades according to their scores, even though they are among the top high school graduates in the state.

Determining the point of functional literacy for reading therefore becomes largely an arbitrary decision accompanied by acceptance of the ambiguity inherent in the very notion of "grade level." This point of functional literacy is usually considered to be somewhat between the fourth and eighth grades (see Carbo, 1987; Chall, Heron, & Hilferty, 1987; Holzman, 1988; Kozol, 1985; McLaren, 1988). In this text, we consider a fourth-grade reading level to represent functional literacy for two reasons. It coincides with the lowest level commonly associated with literacy by reading researchers. In addition, based on our work with young people, we believe this level reflects students' ability to perform the simple decoding acts that serve as a threshold to a range of texts and to the development of higher-level skills.

Implicit in the expression "functional literacy" is the notion that it represents a level of reading and writing that enables people to function in society. Literacy campaigns often garner volunteers and funds by portraying the functionally illiterate as people who cannot participate in mainstream America but must live on the fringes. Books about literacy like Jonathan Kozol's (1985) *Illiterate America* often encourage this perception through vivid depictions of individual illiteracy as a personal tragedy linked with shame and lost social and financial opportunities.

There is some danger of oversimplification in such views, however. American society is sufficiently flexible and diversified to allow those who cannot read and write to function within certain fairly obvious constraints. One would imagine, in fact, that if 60 or even 20 million people actually stopped "functioning" the effects would be visible and severe. Our work with adult illiterates suggests that when they find themselves in situations that require reading and writing, one of three things usually occurs: they remove themselves from the situation; they admit to being illiterate and ask a literate person, say a friend, a clerk, or a secretary, to perform the task for them; or they adopt a strategy that allows them to circumvent the immediate demand. For example, if asked to read something, they may claim to have forgotten their glasses; if asked to write something, as on an application, they may claim to be late for a medical appointment and may request to take the form with them, to be returned later. The point is that they do function, although differently from the way literates do.

In the nation's classrooms, it is possible to observe similar coping strategies. Teachers are often surprised when they discover that a student they have recently graduated cannot read, even though we know that most schools ask students to read and write very little (Goodlad, 1984) and that children who do no work are sometimes passed on from grade to grade on the basis of attendance, if nothing else. Inadequate methods of assessing literacy, combined with students' resourcefulness, can mask serious reading and writing problems.

Some scholars argue that the very structure of society perpetuates functional illiteracy owing to a need for a large pool of unskilled labor to perform menial tasks (see, for example, Giroux, 1983; Graff, 1987). The makeup of the pool may change over time, say from Irish to Italian to Jewish to Hispanic, but the social niche does not. Graff (1987), for example, proposes that public education in the United States has focused primarily on developing ''appropriate'' (as deemed by members of an elite group) forms of social behavior in young people rather than on preparing them vocationally or intellectually. Pointing to the tracking programs that, on and off, have been part of American education for generations, he suggests that throughout this century the forms of school-reinforced behavior have varied according to the particular social class of each group of students. For those from the lower classes, the stress has been on docility, the self-discipline needed to perform repetitive tasks, and respect for authority. For those from the higher classes, it has been on verbal or analytical skills and reasoning ability.

As will become clearer in later chapters, the above discussion is important in determining the goals of literacy instruction among nonnative English-speaking students. Rapid exit into English-only classes, lack of commitment in many schools to developing native-language literacy, an emphasis on teaching subskills that have no correlation with reading and writing performance, and a wide array of institutional biases against such students combine to limit the prospects they may have of attaining high-level literacy skills. That is, all too often functional literacy becomes the schools' tacit educational objective for nonnative English speakers.

Cultural Literacy

Cultural literacy refers to a much broader range of behavior associated with what is seen as the socio-historical context of writing. In this view, meaning is not inherent in discourse; readers and writers *construct it* as they process texts, a point we take up again in Chapter 2. The discourse community in which readers and writers and the texts coexist significantly influences both the form and content of meaning. In other words, people, texts, and meaning do not exist in a vacuum. What a text means depends on what readers bring to the reading or writing, and what they bring will depend on background, training, values, experience, ideology, and so forth.

In this view, readers and writers are linked to the cultural heritage of a given community, an argument made most forcefully in E.D. Hirsch's (1987) book *Cultural Literacy*. Dismissing functional literacy as insufficient in a complex society, Hirsch proposes that literacy must be based on a foundation of shared knowledge and traditions, and he provides a list of terms, events, names of past United States presidents, and literary works that he believes are fundamental to being an educated American.

Hirsch and other advocates of cultural literacy (see Bennett, 1984; Ravitch & Finn, 1988) argue that the United States is experiencing a literacy crisis not because the nation's schools are producing a generation of young people who cannot write or read but because they are failing to perpetuate Western culture.

In Hirsch's account, the connection between culture and literacy is based on two principles of information processing: (1) that comprehensible messages consist of both old or known information and new or unknown information, and (2) that any message consisting completely of new information will be incomprehensible. (Hirsch argued the latter point forcefully in *The Philosophy of Composition*, 1977; also see Quine, 1960, who presents an even more provocative analysis of these principles.) From this perspective, cultural illiteracy is a greater problem than functional illiteracy because the impact is broader, extending beyond texts to oral communication. Without a common foundation of shared experiences and so on, meaningful discourse is impossible. People may exchange words, but they won't *mean* anything.

This insight isn't particularly striking, although the consequences, should they occur, are certainly grim. It reflects the current understanding that literacy cannot be seen as a uniform concept. As we noted previously, in "Perspectives on Literacy," one's degree of literacy is context-dependent: People who can read novels may not be able to read a calculus text. Decoding or processing individual words isn't the problem, but combining them into a meaningful whole is.

The mechanisms that underlie cultural literacy—specifically, the need for people to share some common ground for communication to take place—are straightforward and are not particularly controversial. As far as we can determine, they are accurate. What makes the concept of cultural literacy problematic are the political and ideological factors associated with any attempt to determine *what should constitute the common ground*. For advocates of cultural literacy like Hirsch, it consists of the body of information that history has recognized as being worthy of preservation. Teaching literacy in this context would therefore involve transmitting this body of information to students.

Initially, the "test of time" sounds like a reasonable criterion for determining what should find its way into the common ground of preserved culture. Reflection suggests, however, that it may not be acceptable, because the process is far from objective and is likely to slight those outside the mainstream. History, after all, is not an objective enterprise. As Aronowitz and Giroux (1988) point out:

> Hirsch's view of history is the narrative of the winners. It is the discourse of the elites in history that constitutes the fund of cultural knowledge that defines literacy. . . . Ignorance, for Hirsch, is not merely the absence of information. At stake is *what* the students know. Literacy and illiteracy are defined by the information students possess regarding the canon of knowledge that constitutes the national culture. (p. 184)

Nowhere is the education model inherent in cultural literacy more visible than in the nation's colleges and universities, where entry into the domain of the educated elite is tied to mastery of a shared body of knowledge collectively labeled "the liberal arts." Students are required to take core courses in history, art, literature, and philosophy that supposedly enable them to lead cultured lives.

The model, like cultural literacy itself, is problematic. Historically, professors have always bemoaned the quality of their students, but over the last 20 years faculty have been increasingly distressed by entering students' preparation. The democratization of higher education that began after World War II and accelerated during the Vietnam era brought working-class values and experiences to college campuses, such that the culture of large numbers of freshmen was better reflected in Studs Terkel than in Milton (see Jencks, 1972; Shaughnessey, 1977; Shayer, 1972). It isn't that these students have no cultural experience but that their experience is of a fundamentally different kind than what the liberal arts curriculum is about.

We would argue that too many people confuse cultural literacy with what we call *academic literacy*, the ability to process and interact with a body of artifacts and ideas preserved within the specific domains of educational institutions. It is a set of behaviors peculiar to the formally educated. Academic literacy reflects the notion that literate people are those who read literature, philosophy, history, and contemporary essays, the very sort of texts college students face during their first two years of undergraduate work. It reflects the notion that they can also write about these texts in some fashion. And it reflects the belief that they can comprehend such texts within the larger context of Western cultural traditions that reach back to ancient Greece. For example, someone who is academically literate could be expected to read an article about marathons and associate this modern sporting event with the Battle of Marathon, in which the Greeks fought against the Persians in 490 B.C.

Academic literacy, however, formulates a false sense of culture in its broadest sense: the totality of socially transmitted values, beliefs, thoughts, and behavior patterns characteristic of the nation. Academic literacy is not the culture of the majority of students or their families, nor the culture of blacks or American

Indians or Hispanics. It is the culture of teachers, who quite naturally advocate the supremacy of their own beliefs to the exclusion of others. Merit isn't the primary issue, but hegemony is. For this reason, we find a writer/teacher like Alan Bloom (1987) mourning in *The Closing of the American Mind* the fact that young people prefer Michael Jackson to Mozart. Rock-and-roll, he tells us, is simply a primitive paean to "untutored sexuality." The music isn't bad in and of itself, but it's "primitive" and "sexual," the antithesis to "cultured" and "intellectual" and therefore outside the category of cultural artifact in the narrow sense of "cultivated."

In our view, advocates of academic literacy and any form of cultural literacy that is related to lists of preferred knowledge are misdirected. The consequences of successful advocacy could, we suppose, somehow prove harmful to those whose values and beliefs are excluded from any final list. But the real difficulty lies in the inherent nature of such conceptualizations of literacy to be closed systems.

Closed systems tend to lose their vitality and eventually to disappear. The consequences for education, we believe, are already visible in the huge numbers of students who simply don't like school because it does not seem to relate to their lives. It isn't a matter of making classes more "relevant" but more meaningful. For example, in many high school English classes, the period of modern literature begins around the turn of the century and ends shortly after World War II. The system is closed, which appears to be related to the fact that, when one of this text's authors asked entering freshmen at three major universities how many books they had read for pleasure over the previous year, the average response was zero.

We would suggest that the closed-system status of literacy in our public schools allows teachers to help students learn to read but does not allow them to help students become literate. Literate behavior is linked to making texts personally meaningful, which necessitates a pedagogy of inclusion, not exclusion. As Shirley Heath (1986) notes:

> Literacy does not lead . . . [students] to make the essential leap from literacy to being literate—from knowing what the words say to understanding what they mean. Readers make meaning by linking the symbols on the page with real-world knowledge and then considering what the text means for generating new ideas and actions not explicitly written or "said" in the text. (p. 16)

Without question, increased politicization has in recent years brought a variety of groups—the lower classes, the nonwhite, the foreign born, and women—to challenge the hegemony of academic literacy. Their argument is that it fails to adequately represent nonmainstream culture and that by default it fails to be truly pluralistic in an ever more pluralistic society.

The net result of this challenge has been modest to date, however. Certainly, anthologies for today's students include a larger selection of minority and female writers than did those of 10 years ago. And changes in the way some teachers evaluate writing, focusing on content rather than on surface features, have reduced a few of the difficulties nonnative English speakers have with matters of form as they are developing writing maturity. Yet in some cases, the admission of the historically excluded represents a false concession that fails to alter the status quo. In other cases, the changes are too superficial to reflect any significant broadening of what it means to be academically literate. Academic literacy continues to represent, by and large, texts produced by mainstream males for mainstream males, according to an often rigid application of Standard English.

Although all these issues are intrinsically interesting, from our perspective, which seeks to examine the ways literacy and bilingualism are interrelated, a far more compelling but undeveloped aspect of cultural literacy is how discourse communities influence the ways readers and writers define themselves through the act of engaging in language activities. We know that people use language as a means of social definition, and that reading and writing seem to be important parts of this process. Thus the sorts of things we read and write identify who we are and what our niche is in society. Lawyers, for example, write legal briefs; businesspeople write reports and proposals; professors write textbooks. The framework of cultural literacy allows us to understand how the very tasks we assign nonmainstream students may conflict with the identity they have started to form in their own discourse communities. Traditional reading and writing tasks are inescapably linked to mainstream identities that our language-minority students may feel very uncomfortable with. We explore these ideas more fully in the next chapter.

Critical Literacy

The concept of critical literacy emerged over the last several years largely as a challenge to the common view of cultural literacy as advocated by writers like Hirsch. In its broadest sense, critical literacy denotes not only the ability to recognize the social essence of literacy but also to understand its fundamentally political nature.

For example, when discussing functional literacy, we noted that some writers estimate that perhaps as many as 40 to 60 million adults in America are illiterate. The nation's schools and literacy campaigns commonly approach the problem as though reading and writing skills are commodities that illiterates can simply take home with them, provided they have some degree of motivation and have access to a person willing to give them the goods. Often ignored is the fact that at least half of these people are women and that a large portion of the remainder are immigrants who aren't fluent in English (Rockhill, 1987). That is, the majority of the country's functional illiterates are members of two politically disenfranchised groups. The commodities view fails to take into account how literacy, as patterns of behavior, is embedded in a complex social context that includes a full range of power relationships. Those who have a voice in their community receive what they ask for. Those without a voice can't even ask.

From this perspective, advocates of cultural literacy who argue for a shared body of knowledge as the foundation for becoming literate are striving, consciously or not, to exclude everyone who is not part of the mainstream. For those on the periphery, becoming literate in the traditional curriculum may require forsaking nonmainstream cultural values and yielding to docile tokenism or rejecting the curriculum and expressing rebellion by dropping out. Freire and Macedo (1987) suggest, on this account, that the high dropout rate among blacks and Hispanics in the United States is the result of their refusal to participate in an educational process that attempts to replace their cultural values with those of the Anglo-European mainstream.

The ideology of academic literacy is seen to oppress not only minority students but minority texts. Freire and Macedo (1987) and Cummins (1988), for example, argue that the texts students read in school are those that do not threaten the status quo. Elaborating on this argument, McLaren (1988) states: "Works by writers who have been marginalized because they happen to be female or members of minority groups, or works that constitute political perspectives inhospitable to the dominant culture are not likely to be admitted to the national canon" (p. 225).

We would suggest that an equally important feature of critical literacy consists of the developed ability to assess the ideology of individual texts. As such, it would represent the highest level of literacy skills in a continuum that begins with the threshold skills of functional literacy. The representative behavior would go beyond recognition of a text's political nature to identifying the specific elements that express it and the writer's ideological perspective.

For example, critically literate readers of John Steinbeck's (1939) *Grapes of Wrath* would first recognize that the text offers more than just an interesting story, that it makes a political statement about America during the Depression. They would then determine on the basis of the Jode family's struggle to survive the move to California that the statement is largely socialistic.

As this example illustrates, this feature of critical literacy is quite dependent on cultural literacy. In addition, it is highly rhetorical because it stresses understanding the intended audience as well as the aim and purpose inherent in a text. Critical literacy on this level involves determining what effect a writer is attempting to bring about in readers, why he or she is making the effort, and just who those readers are.

CONCLUSION

The complexities associated with literacy may initially seem irrelevant to the teachers (perhaps the majority) who merely want to help their children become better readers and writers. Daily classroom reality involves decoding and comprehension, not ideologies per se.

We believe it is important, however, for teachers to understand that their conceptualizations of literacy and thus their strategies for developing students' literacy are inescapably influenced by cultural as well as political concerns. In addition, we believe it is important for teachers to understand that their goal in teaching students to read and write cannot justifiably be simply functional literacy, that they must view basic skills as a threshold for the more complex ones students need, not only for further academic success but for personal growth.

In our view, language is a social action that defines individuals as well as communities. It also defines hierarchical relationships, particularly in those schools with large numbers of nonnative English-speaking students. Only through understanding the complexities involved can teachers begin to change the language of literacy from one of exclusion to one of inclusion. As we discuss in the next chapter, a teacher's view of what literacy is can significantly influence not only teaching methods but expected outcomes as well.

CHAPTER 2

Understanding Reading and Writing

OVERVIEW

Understanding the complex relationships among reading, writing, and bilingualism involves examining the mechanisms of literacy in a way that illuminates how people come to read and write competently in any language. Such an examination will form the foundation for teaching all students whose first language may or may not be English, and it will inform how to enhance literacy skills.

This chapter provides an introduction to reading instruction, outlining two views of how people read: one is a "bottom-up" process, the other "top-down." In addition, it analyzes the teaching strategies associated with these views—the *sight-vocabulary* approach, *phonics*, and the *whole-language* approach.

What emerges is a model of the reading process that emphasizes the importance of context and students' experiences in making meaning. This model is antithetical to the view commonly associated with functional literacy, where reading is deemed a linear process that consists simply of decoding words. It advocates the notion that the goal of reading is to comprehend texts.

At the heart of the model is the perception that meaning is a construction and not something that exists on the page independent of readers and the society they belong to. The chapter therefore outlines the mechanisms involved in this construction, focusing on the role of *short-term*, *working*, and *long-term* memory. In this analysis, working memory matches potential meanings with nonverbal mental models of experience through a process of hypothesis testing. When readers achieve a match, they accept the hypothesized meaning as the actual meaning and are able to comprehend the text.

The process of constructing meaning is not unconstrained, however. Reading, like speaking and writing, is a social action, so social factors significantly influence what meanings readers ascribe to texts. Building on the discussion of cultural literacy in Chapter 1, we suggest that there exists a public dimension to text meaning. This dimension restricts how readers understand texts because they are part of a discourse community with which they have numerous things in common, in addition to language.

The chapter then examines how these views of language influence teaching practices, specifically analyzing how a bottom-up approach to reading instruction can have negative, long-term effects on students as writers. The alternative to this approach emphasizes a whole-language curriculum and the social nature of writing, suggesting an environment where students engage in group work and collaborative learning.

TWO VIEWS OF HOW PEOPLE READ

The theories teachers accept regarding the nature of language influence the ways they help students become literate. As we note here and in succeeding chapters, some widespread theories that describe certain aspects of the relationship between literacy and bilingualism are not particularly sound, yet they continue to affect instruction. For example, ideas about how people read significantly influence how teachers go about teaching reading (see Kroskrity, 1987).

The most common approaches to teaching reading in our schools are *sight-vocabulary* instruction and *phonics*. Sight instruction attempts to teach children random lists of words, usually with flash cards. As the teacher flashes a card, students pronounce it; when they can't, the teacher reads the word. The students go through the cards repeatedly, until they have memorized them, as evidenced by their ability to pronounce each word presented. This approach is popular among many English-as-a-Second-Language (ESL) teachers who believe that the key to students' English proficiency lies largely in increasing their vocabulary. Phonics instruction, on the other hand, consists of teaching children the sounds of the alphabet so they can "sound out" unfamiliar words during reading.

Its widespread use notwithstanding, many researchers dismiss sight instruction because it presents words without a context, which makes meaning and comprehension highly problematic, and because it presupposes that children utilize lists of words when reading, storing individual words in a hypothetical memory bin and pulling them out when needed. It presumes that readers build up meaning on the basis of single words. The idea is that reading comprehension is analogous to an adding machine: people add up the individual words and then get some sort of total that equals meaning. It assumes that what stands in the way of greater comprehension is an insufficient number of words stored in memory, so its explicit goal is to increase the amount of storage (Gibson & Levin, 1975; Goodman, 1967, 1973; F. Smith, 1972, 1983). As we show in the next section, people just don't seem to read this way.

Phonics is perhaps more widely used than sight instruction, and it is probably more controversial. Educators and researchers who advocate this approach argue that the best way to teach reading is through the systematic teaching of phonics, and they argue that success in reading depends on accurately identifying words and the sounds of words through a process known as "decoding" (see, for example, Chall, 1983; Flesch, 1955; Fries, 1962; Mathews, 1966; J.P. Williams, 1979). Other researchers disagree, however, arguing that successful reading is more complicated than phonics advocates recognize (Adams, 1987; Bewley, 1987; Fritz, 1987; Henry, 1987; Philips, 1988). Henry (1987), for example, studying elementary students, found that phonics instruction developed rudimentary reading skill but that, ironically, it produced little knowledge about the structure of words or word patterns. A large body of recent research like that cited above indicates, in fact, that reading entails predicting and synthesizing meaning primarily on the basis of syntax, context, intention, and purpose, not phonics.

This debate is important to our discussion of literacy not only because it deals with the mechanisms of reading and comprehension but because of the growing awareness that reading and writing are closely linked (see Dobson, 1988; Flower, 1988; Mason, 1988). We can see quite clearly how revision and editing, two significant parts of writing performance, are tied to the writer's role as reader. More important, however, is the perception that the behaviors teachers reinforce in young readers transfer to the behaviors these students adopt as writers (Beach & Liebeman-Kleine, 1986; Self, 1986), a point we examine in the section, "How Theory Influences Practice: The Consequences of Error Correction," later in this chapter.

A Model of the Reading Process

The nature of the debate can be better understood if these two competing models of how people read are analyzed in more detail. In the phonics model, comprehension begins with the print on the page. It proposes that, when reading a sentence or paragraph, people perceive words as individual letters, which they combine into syllables. They then join the syllables into whole words. Through a cumulative process, they combine the words into phrases and clauses and the phrases and clauses into sentences.

In this view, the meaning of sentences and paragraphs is determined from the meaning of the individual words that comprise them. Also, individual word meanings are believed to be derived on the basis on sound, suggesting not only a direct sound-to-symbol correspondence for words, but also a direct correspondence between the sound of a word and its meaning. This conceptualization of reading, going from letters to meaning, is usually referred to as an example of a *bottom-up* model of cognitive processing.

Although the phonics model may initially appear to be an accurate representation of the reading process, closer consideration reveals some serious problems. Do readers, for example, derive textual meaning on the basis of a sound-to-symbol correspondence? Proposing they do reduces the unit of meaning from the word to the phoneme, which seems counter-intuitive. Some phonemes, such as participles like "ing" and "ed," do in fact convey meaning, as demonstrated by the difference in meaning of "Fred was drown*ing*" and "Fred drown*ed*." But most don't seem to do so at all. Moreover, English doesn't have a very impressive sound-to-symbol correspondence. That is, the letters in the alphabet are not really associated with the phonemes or sounds they are supposed to represent.

For example, what is the sound of the letter /b/? Is it "be" as in "begin," or is it "buh" as in "book"? Or, as this example illustrates, is it both? The fact that there are other sounds also associated with the letter /b/ is significantly confusing to adults and is likely to be even more so to children. The case of consonant clusters, such as /gh/, of course presents even greater difficulties for the phonics model.

It's easy enough to show that the meaning of individual words more often than not depends upon syntax, context, and knowledge about how the world operates, not on spelling. In fact, there is significant research that suggests the bottom-up processing model does not correctly depict actual language endeavors in their totality but only a small part of what people do (see Abbott, Black, & Smith, 1985; Fodor, Bever, & Garrett, 1974; Kintsch & van Dijk, 1978; Malt, 1985; Schank & Abelson, 1977; Warren & Warren, 1970).

The model we endorse as an alternative to phonics, comprehension by synthesis, is based on such research. For example, our understanding of the sentences below is clearly not the result of a bottom-up process:

1. Maria put the *hose* in the garage.
2. Ted wanted to *hose* off the sidewalk.
3. Juanita found a run in her *hose*.
4. The policemen used a rubber *hose* on the suspect.

Comprehending these sentences and differentiating the meaning of *hose* in each clearly involves not just knowing the meanings of the individual words but also knowing something about how the world operates. The individual meanings of *hose* depend on this knowledge. On the basis of these sentences, we begin to understand that meaning comes not so much from combining letters into the word (from bottom up) as from applying knowledge of the world to this particular word (from top down). Writers like Johnson-Laird (1983), Sanford and Garrod (1981), and F. Smith (1983) therefore conclude that reading is primarily a *top-down* process. We would suggest, however, that reading and most other linguistic acts involve interactive processes. That is, they operate in both a bottom-up and a top-down manner.

Johnson-Laird (1983) suggests that top-down information processing relies on the development of mental models that describe how the world functions. To a large extent, these models will be linked to previous experiences and the sort of shared knowledge characterized in our discussion of cultural literacy in Chapter 1. We're able to distinguish the four different meanings of the word *hose* in the sentences above, for example, because we're able to construct separate mental models for each based on what we know. Hence, in a discourse community where, say, hosiery doesn't exist, sentence (3) above would be meaningless.

Mental models develop from and are elaborated through experience, and in their most rudimentary form they may not even be verbal but may consist of representational or logical relationships. Consider sentence (4): As you read it, do you visualize a scene that includes a suspect bound to a chair, a bright light in his face, and a beefy policeman, perhaps a cigar stub in the corner of his mouth, with a short piece of rubber hose in one hand? The words in the sentence evoke this scene, this model, but they are not exclusively associated with it; the model exists in our minds independent of this particular sentence. *Reading and writing therefore may be thought of as processes by which representational or logical relationships, in the form of mental models, are matched with words that convey the meaning of those relationships.*

Currently, this model of the reading process appears to be the most viable. It fits most of what we know about language development, literacy acquisition, and cognitive processing. Applying this model involves a whole-language approach to literacy, which stresses the reciprocal, interactive aspects of the four language modes: reading, writing, listening, and speaking. We will examine this approach closely in later chapters, but here we will note that it engages students in language activities that combine two or more of these modes. Students may begin a writing task, for example, by first creating the "text" orally for teacher and fellow students. After receiving feedback, they may then write the text, which may become the basis for a reading activity.

This model can also help teachers better understand some of the factors that will influence their work in teaching reading and writing in the bilingual/multilingual classroom. It suggests that people may formulate meaningful relationships but may not have the verbal tools necessary to convey them to others. It also suggests that for comprehension to occur between writers and readers, their mental models of the relationship being described must match.

When students are working in their primary language, it is less likely that a mismatch will occur, but occasionally one does. In this event, they will reject their initial mental model and try a different one until a match is achieved or until they give up and classify the discourse as incomprehensible.

But if the speaker/hearer or the writer/reader come from very different linguistic and cultural backgrounds, as is the case in bilingual classes when students are working with texts in the second language, there are various obstacles to achieving a match. We must stress that we are not talking simply about problems related to different "codes," that is, vocabulary and grammar. Not only might experiences differ, but the motivation for relating those experiences might differ, in which case the rationale for communication and for the matching of mental models will be at cross purposes (see Heath, 1983).

Some cultures, for example, emphasize the functional aspects of objects, whereas others do not. From a functional perspective, tables and chairs are similar because they are used for dining, not because they have four legs; a forest is a source of lumber and food, not a nature preserve, and so forth.

Students from a culture that focuses on function are therefore likely to have trouble comprehending a piece of writing that describes an object in an abstract, nonfunctional way, as most school texts do. Equally important, such students are also likely to have difficulty with writing assignments that ask them to produce this same sort of description.

Matching mental models when processing discourse involves *hypothesis testing*. When reading, we formulate certain hypotheses regarding the meaning of a text and then test those hypotheses against the text itself. For example, if you picked up a book titled, say, *Southwest Cooking*, you would perhaps hypothesize that it is a cookbook, with recipes for dishes popular in the Southwest. When you opened the book and glanced through it, you would be confirming or disconfirming that hypothesis, since the book might not be a cookbook at all.

Teachers of students outside mainstream American culture need to be aware that a significant part of successful hypothesis testing is the result of being able to formulate appropriate categories that serve to describe experiences. Our cookbook example, for instance, required that we have a category for objects called "cookbooks"; we determined whether *Southwest Cooking* fit into that category. Teachers cannot, however, assume that language-minority students will possess the same categories for their experiences that they have. Not all students will have a category, say, for cookbooks (see Lakoff, 1987).

COMPREHENSION AS A CONSTRUCTIVE PROCESS

As readers look at the words on a page of text, they are engaged in an intentional activity. That is, they have a reason for reading; they may be doing what their teacher told them to do or following the directions on a TV dinner. Their purpose for reading will significantly influence not only the strategies they use but how much they remember.

We know from studies of how the eyes move during reading that people don't look at every word on the page. Instead, they process lines of text into clusters of three to seven words, depending on their verbal fluency and the difficulty of the text (Clark & Clark, 1977; F. Smith, 1972). The eyes make sweeping arcs across the page, usually pausing at what are called "constituent boundaries," which we can think of not only as the ends of sentences but as places where clauses and phrases come together in sentences. Very skilled readers, however, often show additional, sometimes random, patterns of eye movement; they will characteristically skip sentences, read sentences backwards, and loop back from one sentence to an earlier one (see Gibson & Levin, 1975).

We have to conclude from such studies that reading for comprehension is far from being the completely linear process that many people believe it is. Skilled readers use the words on the pages as cues to formulate a representation of the whole text. They spend very little energy decoding single words.

Reaching some understanding of just what goes on during reading requires the use of a hypothetical description of the various components involved in comprehending written language. According to a widely accepted model (see Baddeley, 1986; Johnson-Laird, 1983; Perfetti & Curtis, 1966; Shankweiler & Crain, 1986), as the eyes pause at points in the text, word clusters enter a temporary storage area that we can call "short-term memory." They are held here for a fraction of a second while a cognitive process evaluates whether they are useful to the reader's purpose for processing the text.

If they are deemed useful, they go into what we can call "working memory," where the actual construction of meaning appears to take place. The entire cluster is interpreted as a unit, and the potential meaning of the unit is matched against a broad set of logical relationships and internal representations of reality stored more or less permanently in "long-term memory." The meaning is "potential" until the matching process is completed because it exists only as a hypothesis of what the unit may actually mean. For ambiguous sentences, such as "Jim put the toy in the box on the shelf," readers will have two models to match the input against, and they will rely on the context to match the correct one to a single meaning. If there is indeed a match, the potential meaning is accepted as a "proposition" (see Figure 2.1). If there is no match, the proposition is labeled "incomprehensible" (although not necessarily meaningless) and is usually discarded.

Once meaning is constructed through hypothesis testing, the cluster itself is purged to accommodate another incoming one. The first proposition may be stored immediately in long-term memory if it is complete, or it may be stored temporarily in working memory if it is incomplete, to await processing of the newly arrived word cluster.

We can illustrate this mechanism with the following sentences:

5. Dogs bark.
6. In the morning, I ate breakfast.

The first sentence could be processed as a single unit, and because it's complete, its proposition would go directly into long-term storage. Let's pro-

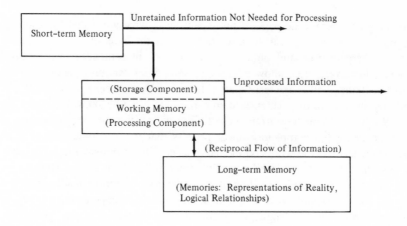

Figure 2.1. Representation of Memory during Text Processing

pose, however, that with (6) we break the sentence into two units at the comma. We would first process "In the morning," but there are two textual cues signaling that more remains to be done. The first is the punctuation, and the second is the lack of agent and action. We would therefore hold the proposition in working memory until "I ate breakfast" is processed. Then the two units would be joined into a single proposition and stored in long-term memory. This process repeats, in one form or another, depending on the number of propositions in the text, until readers accomplish their purpose, which often cannot be equated with reaching the end of the text.

It's important to stress that comprehension involves a two-way mechanism between long-term memory and working memory. For comprehension to take place, readers must have a range of logical relationships and internal representations of reality to associate with potential meaning. If they are lacking such relationships and representations, the text will be largely incomprehensible. In very simple terms this principle indicates, as suggested in Chapter 1, that readers can only comprehend texts that they already know quite a bit about.

It is in this area that our language-minority students may experience much difficulty if they are asked to begin their English reading with texts unrelated to what they know. They may be able to understand the individual words, but they may not be able to comprehend whole texts because they are likely to lack the relevant mental models needed to process them.

Our analysis does not imply, however, that learning—the formulation of more logical relationships and mental models—cannot take place. But it does reinforce our view that new information and skills must be built on old information and skills. Students acquire the new by associating it with the old, making connections, additions, and modifications.

SOCIAL ASPECTS OF COMPREHENSION

Over the last several years, the constructive nature of comprehension has been interpreted as indicating that a text can mean just about anything a reader wants it to and that the potential meaning of any text is therefore essentially limitless. This view is known as *conventionalism*, and it proposes that one cannot exhaust all the available analyses of meaning (see Iser, 1980). The range of possible interpretations is unlimited because meaning is relative to the individual mind processing the discourse (see Dillon, 1981).

The position of conventionalism appears to ignore the fact that there are powerful constraints on interpretation that make relativity a measurable factor only in cases of ambiguity, which is itself highly constrained, rarely going beyond two possible interpretations. Of these constraints, social restrictions, along with syntactic and pragmatic ones, are among the more significant. Discussing speech, Brown and Yule (1983), for example, suggest that language users "locate themselves in a multi-dimensional space in relation to the rest of their society, and locate each act of speaking in a multidimensional space relative to the rest of their social lives" (p. 83). In their view, language *is* shared culture, since it is learned from other people in a linguistic community; language is thus an intrinsically social activity because it is impossible for a normal person to produce discourse that cannot be understood by another who shares the language and the discourse community.

We would suggest here, as in our discussion of cultural literacy, that a similar range of social factors is related to comprehension in ways that constrain the meaning of texts and how we comprehend them. As Frege (1977) and others (Brown & Yule, 1983; Levinson, 1983) argue, there is a public dimension to text meaning. That is, we understand texts because they are part of a discourse community with which we have things in common, *in addition to the language*. If we have nothing in common with the community a text belongs to, it will be incomprehensible (see Quine, 1960).

It is important to understand, however, that reading a text links readers to specific communities. For example, reading an art book links readers to the community of art, a cookbook to the community of cooks, a history book to the community being described. In many instances, the link is so strong that the reading experience acts as a catalyst to draw readers further into the community. Martha Stewart's cookbooks have motivated many people over the last few years to strive to identify themselves as gourmet cooks. Exercise books motivate people to jog, practice aerobics, change their diets, and so forth. (Other media have a similar effect: some years ago, after release of the movie *The Paper Chase*, which was about being a law student at Harvard, law school applications increased dramatically, even though the experience was depicted very negatively.)

We would therefore argue that the community mediates comprehension, that it influences the meaning readers can construct for any given text. It does so in a number of ways, the most obvious being its nature as the source of most of our internal representations of reality. Our interactions with others tell us a great deal about how the world operates. On another level, however, society serves as a sounding board to help confirm or disconfirm the hypotheses we make about a text's meaning. That is, we construct a representation of what a text means, and then we ask the community to tell us if we're right or wrong. This process is particularly prevalent in schools, of course, and indeed is built into the very fabric of nearly all learning activities. In this respect, schools function significantly to socialize comprehension, accepting some readings of texts but not others.

The idea of socialized comprehension has significant implications for reading activities in the classroom. On the positive side, it suggests that by carefully selecting reading materials teachers can encourage cultural literacy among language-minority students. Some texts can serve to affirm the cultural identities of the students, helping them define themselves and their home communities. Others can introduce students to the nuances of mainstream American culture and help them identify with its institutions.

We see the consequences of this understanding most clearly in efforts to provide reading materials that depict minorities and women performing jobs that traditionally have been the domain of mainstream white males. We would suggest, however, that such efforts represent merely a first step and may inappropriately focus exclusively on economic status.

On the negative side, we may find that older students, especially, can be inclined to experience some anxiety when dealing with texts that implicitly ask them to identify with the mainstream. There is a sense in which reading a text involves accepting the writer's representation of reality as one's own. This is part of the power of language. Yet older students are more aware of the social barriers that hinder assimilation, and they recognize that stronger association with the mainstream community frequently results in weakening ties with the home and its community. As as result, many may feel a conflict.

In addition, texts generally rely on social and cultural premises to cue meaning. A middle school text about an adolescent testing the limits of her personal freedom with her parents, for example, may be largely incomprehensible to students from cultures that place more value on respecting parents and less on individuality—not because they fail to understand the words or even the sentences, but because they fail to grasp the cultural value Americans place on individuality. And it is this social factor that shapes the meaning of the text.

Teachers need to be aware that asking students to read engages them in an activity that is far more complex than it may initially appear. They are not simply decoding words. They are dealing with a range of social factors that will influence not only what they want to read but how well they comprehend it. We would suggest that in this respect reading is just as much a social action as speaking and writing. It helps young people define who they are and how they fit into a variety of communities.

HOW THEORY INFLUENCES PRACTICE:
THE CONSEQUENCES OF ERROR CORRECTION

A characteristic feature of phonics reading instruction is that it focuses on error correction, with problematic results. Typically, beginning reading in the classroom is done aloud, because it allows the teacher to monitor student progress. Such monitoring can be valuable if used properly; the teacher can observe children's reading strategies and then work individually with them to improve comprehension. But what we frequently find, especially in multilingual classrooms, is that reading becomes for students a process of merely pronouncing words accurately, with the teacher correcting them when they make mistakes.

To understand the consequences of such error correction more fully, one must recognize that it is extremely difficult for even proficient readers to comprehend a passage if they are being stopped and corrected every few words. Attention is interrupted, and reading speed decreases.

Teachers frequently overlook the fact that interruptions make comprehension difficult, even though there is general agreement among researchers that reading speed is correlated with understanding. This correlation explains why students in remedial reading programs often are trained to increase their speed, usually with the aid of reading machines.

The importance of speed is related to how the mind processes and stores information. As we noted previously in this chapter, good readers break sentences into phrases that go into short-term memory. It's widely believed that meaning is not a feature of short-term memory; the clusters of words are simply held for a brief period and then integrated into propositions in working memory (see Baddeley, 1986; Shankweiler & Crain, 1986).

Short-term memory has a limited capacity and is easily overloaded. Few people can hold more than seven bits of information in short-term memory without some deterioration. When teachers interrupt students' reading to correct errors, reading proceeds on the basis of words rather than phrases, and attention is on words rather than meaning. As a result, each word is held in short-term memory until memory capacity is reached, at which point a new incoming word displaces one of those being held. This sort of overload has been demonstrated to severely impair comprehension, so correcting students' errors when they read is just not good pedagogy (see Clark & Clark, 1977; Malt, 1985).

Nevertheless, teachers working with bilingual students may object that comprehension cannot occur if a child reads a passage and commits numerous errors along the way. The individual errors must add up to errors in comprehension. As it turns out, this is actually not the case.

Reading aloud without practicing the passage in advance is quite difficult for all readers, so we should expect errors when we ask our students to read. Even experienced readers make errors when reading texts they haven't rehearsed. Goodman (1973) has termed such errors *miscues* (also see Watson, 1985). Miscues can be classified into four types, listed below by frequency of occurrence and with corresponding examples:

Type	*Printed Text/Uttered Text*
1. substitution	the beautiful woman/ the *bella* woman
2. omission	a wet, ugly dog/a wet dog
3. insertion	sent me a book/sent to me a book
4. scramble	the boys ran/they all ran

When children read aloud, teachers generally see miscues as evidence of poor skill, so they interrupt to correct the "error," asking students to reread the word. Several studies have shown, however, that most miscues preserve the meaning of the passage, as in (1) above, so such error correction seems of limited value (see Gibson & Levin, 1975; Weber, 1968). Gibson and Levin (1975) report that 90 percent of substitution errors preserve the meaning of the text. If meaning is preserved, there seems no reason to make a correction. In the event the miscue does not preserve meaning, there is evidence suggesting that children will stop and reread the passage, making the correction themselves if given the chance (see Gibson & Levin, 1975; F. Smith, 1983).

This analysis shouldn't be construed as advocating sloppiness or carelessness; we want students to develop an appreciation for accuracy in language. But an *overconcern* with word accuracy hinders comprehension. Moreover, among bilingual students it can create performance anxiety that may have long-term effects on academic achievement. Such anxiety interferes with learning because learning involves risk taking. Children who are so afraid of failure that they refuse to take risks will not learn very quickly and most likely will not find learning particularly pleasant (see Harter, 1981).

Reading and Writing: Making Connections

In our analysis, we must consider the fact that huge numbers of students learn to read using a bottom-up approach like phonics instruction. Moreover, studies of reading performance indicate that during the first two years of instruction students who learn to read through phonics seem to outperform students who learn to read using a top-down, whole-language approach (see Beck, 1984; Ehri, 1983; Perfetti & Curtis, 1986). But at the end of two years, the performance difference begins to disappear until the two groups are reading at comparable levels.

Given such data, why should teachers concern themselves with the two reading models we've been describing? We would suggest that the consequences of error correction in reading are long-term and that they significantly affect *writing*. Stopping and correcting students who miscue "beautiful" and substitute *bella* forces them to attend to the surface features of the text. The text's meaning, as well as its rhetorical features, necessarily become secondary. And if children are trained to read texts in this way, it seems unlikely that they will approach reading their own writing any differently.

We can, in fact, predict that such students will be inclined to concentrate on surface correctness rather than on global features associated with meaning. Not only will they find writing unpleasant, but their writing will lack the rhetorical features that essentially comprise the cues for comprehension. Their written sentences may not even be grammatical because they fail to recognize, and thus to utilize, something as basic as syntactic cues (Betancourt & Phinney, 1988; Daly, 1977; Edelsky, 1982; Jacobs, 1985; Krashen, 1982). Furthermore, it isn't common for bilingual students to engage in a "what-next?" strategy with writing that manages to get words on the page, but without much organization or direction. In response to these problems, various researchers have been suggesting for some time that the real problem with nonmainstream writing is the lack of organization and elaboration needed to communicate a meaningful message, not the lack of surface correctness (Edelsky, 1986; Farr & Daniels, 1986).

Skill Sequencing

Typically, students are taught to write after they have learned to read, and the instruction they receive resembles reading instruction. Students initially practice writing the alphabet, then individual words; later these individual words are combined into simple sentences, which eventually are combined into paragraphs, and so on. Even much university writing instruction focuses on sentences and paragraphs rather than essays, in the belief that work with isolated sentences will lead to better compositions. Many scholars, however, are beginning to agree that it is better to have students write whole compositions, not small pieces of them (see J.D. Williams, 1989).

The influence of a bottom-up model in the sentence/paragraph approach is fairly obvious, but it's important to understand how notions of sequencing learning activities have shaped the curriculum. When writing instruction follows reading instruction, it suggests that the language modes are distinct and different: the second activity is built on the first. But all language activities are essentially similar, whether listening, speaking, reading, or writing. Utterances and texts are alike in a fundamental way—they are social actions used to make requests, supply information, make assertions, and ask and answer questions.

Over the last few years, growing numbers of teachers have recognized the importance of an integrated approach to language instruction for all students. They aim at emphasizing the functional nature of school discourse. The result has been a shift—admittedly modest in many districts—away from the transitional language arts sequence to a more integrated curriculum, one that not only implements the sort of whole-language approach mentioned earlier but that also draws on students' experiences and linguistic/rhetorical knowledge to enhance learning.

A significant feature of the whole-language approach is the emphasis on collaborative learning strategies that encourage group work. Students in groups become partly responsible for one another's success or failure. Thus some teachers may, for example, begin writing tasks by having students develop their essays orally in work groups, utilizing oral discourse strategies to reinforce student's compositions. Then reading activities focus on texts that the students have produced, not on professional texts, so writing and reading are intimately linked. The grammar drills and exercises so often associated with writing instruction for nonnative English-speaking students largely disappear.

Using Text Models to Improve Writing

Most teachers working with junior and senior high school students still use published texts as models for students to imitate when they write. Several years of observing bilingual classrooms convinces us that too much time that should be devoted to writing instruction is actually spent either working through exercises and drills on surface features or going over text models. As a result, students do very little writing.

Several assumptions govern the use of models. One is that reading and writing are interrelated in a way that makes the skills involved in each task mutually transferable. That is, if students can read a sophisticated, complex sentence, they should be able to write one. Another assumption is that knowing what characterizes good writing enables students to produce good writing on their own. Finally, reading and/or analyzing examples of good writing is assumed to produce such knowledge.

Part of the rationale for these assumptions is our intuitive awareness that students must have at least some genre familiarity in order to manipulate writing's formal conventions. For example, it would be very difficult to write a haiku poem without ever having actually seen and analyzed one. We know that many of the formal conventions found in writing, such as explicit cohesive ties like "however" and "therefore," are rarely found in conversational speech, and we know that the students' internalized models for these conventions must come from somewhere. Experience with reading appears to be the only reasonable source.

Several studies seem to support these assumptions. Donelson (1967) examined essays from "effective" and "ineffective" tenth-grade writers, comparing evaluations on three of their essays and correlating these with self-reports of reading activity. He found that the "effective" writers reported reading more than the "ineffective" writers. Woodward and Phillips (1967) conducted a similar investigation using college freshmen. As in the Donelson study, the good writers reported reading relatively more than the poor ones. Kimberling, Wingate, Rosser, and Krashen (cited in Krashen, 1978) replicated these earlier investigations and likewise found a significant correlation between reading history and writing performance.

Additional, more rigorous research on this question avoided the problems inherent in questionnaire surveys, and it obtained similar results. Thibodeau (1964), working with sixth-graders, Reedy (1966), with ninth-graders, and Stefl (1981), with third-graders, established treatment and control groups and used brief passages selected to model specific characteristics of good prose. Students in the treatment groups were presented with the models for analysis, whereas students in the control groups were not. In each case, the treatment groups demonstrated significant gains in writing performance over the control groups.

In an effort to explain such findings from a linguistic point of view, Steve Krashen (1981b, 1985) proposes that writing performance is directly influenced by a person's reading history, arguing that reading provides the "meaningful input" required for literacy acquisition. He calls this the *reading hypothesis*.

Krashen's insight into the nature of literacy acquisition is quite sound. He outlines a process by which young people are immersed in texts and thereby unconsciously acquire the structural and rhetorical models that underlie written discourse. Unfortunately, his formulation of the reading hypothesis is problematic for several reasons. He argues, for example, that a person's reading experience must not only be intensive and self-motivated but that it must occur during adolescence. He also argues for a strong cause-effect relationship, that is, that those who read extensively will be good writers. We know, however, that early reading experience is important to literacy acquisition. Recent research indicates, for example, that literacy success may be influenced as early as age 3 by textual awareness and reading strategies. (Jackson, Donaldson, & Cleland, 1988). We also know that many people read voluminously but are poor writers (see Johnson & Louis, 1985; J.D. Williams, 1989).

Moreover, the hypothesis does not sufficiently account for the role writing plays in literacy acquisition. Literacy acquisition requires immersion in both reading and writing; reading alone is not enough to develop competent literacy skills.

It is perhaps this last factor that explains a large body of research that, contrary to the studies outlined above, reports no significant correlation between text models and writing performance. W. Clark (1968), for example, studied two groups of college students in an effort to determine possible relationships between reading and writing. One group analyzed models, while the other group did not. At the end of the study, there was no significant difference in writing between the groups, based on holistic evaluation of pretreatment and posttreatment writing samples. Lareau (1971) and Perry (1980), also working with college students, used similar methods and reported no significant differences between groups.

Among elementary and secondary students, various studies using models under controlled conditions failed to demonstrate any significant differences between treatment and control groups (see Caplan & Keech, 1980; Martin, 1981; Pinkham, 1969; Sponsler, 1971; Vinson, 1980; West, 1967). In light of the fact that some controlled studies do demonstrate a significant effect for models, it seems that at best we can conclude only that the empirical results related to using models to improve writing performance are mixed.

Explaining why text modeling is not more effective is difficult and of necessity must be speculative. We would suggest, however, that being able to analyze a text and describe its structure is a fundamentally different task from producing a text with a similar structure. For example, a person may appreciate Mozart and may even be able to read music, but there is no reason to expect him or her to be able to compose a symphony. It therefore seems unreasonable to propose that textual analysis per se will lead to improved writing performance.

For junior and senior high students it may very well be that models come too little too late. It may also be that they are so abstract that they are simply difficult to internalize, through either acquisition or learning. One may initially object to this idea on the grounds that many aspects of language, such as grammar, are equally abstract and yet are acquired by virtually everyone, regardless of intelligence. We should keep in mind, however, that something like grammar is embedded in a highly meaningful, concrete, functional context. Generally speaking, text models are not.

How the lack of such a context affects literacy acquisition in the classroom can be better understood if we consider what Philip Johnson-Laird (1983) calls the "principle of structural identity." He tells us that "The structures of mental models are identical to the structures of the states of affairs, whether perceived or conceived, that the models represent" (p. 419). If this principle is valid, and we have every reason to believe it is, we must ask how abstract textual relations, such as tone, audience, purpose, and so forth, are represented in the mind. How are these rhetorical features represented in a mental model? For that matter, how are they represented in the discourse model the student is asked to imitate and ultimately internalize?

In truth, we don't really know at this point. Scholars are still working to identify and describe precisely the various parts of a composition that establish and convey global features (see van Dijk, 1980). Furthermore, in most instances we can't even perceive abstract relations, only the conditions that count as evidence that they exist. As a result, transferring mental models of concrete relations to abstract ones is extremely difficult. Students given a model essay will be able to recognize that it has a purpose, because the fact that it is published counts as evidence that some purpose exists. They may even be successful in identifying that purpose. But neither of these occurrences means that they will necessarily be able to write a purposeful essay on their own.

Moreover, for the principles of acquisition to work, students need opportunities to read, but not pressure to read. We would therefore suggest that text models should not be the focus of writing tasks. It seems that free reading periods work best to develop a good relationship between students and texts. A wide range of reading materials is a continually updated classroom library is one of the more effective ways to generate this relationship.

WRITING AS A PROCESS IN A SOCIAL CONTEXT

Anyone who would teach should know that language is not simply a tool for communication. It is, especially for children, a means of "social definition." Using language to interact with others, children discover who they are and how they fit into a complex social structure (see Clark & Clark, 1977).

Too often teachers approach writing instruction in a way that ignores the social aspect of language. They focus instead on drills, exercises, and grammatical terminology in the hope that teaching students to label nouns and verbs in sentences will somehow help them write better (see Farr & Daniels, 1986). If students have a writing assignment, they work on it by themselves, either in class or at home, and turn it in for a grade. The teacher takes the papers home, marks all the surface errors (usually in red ink), making abbreviated marginal notes (AMB for *ambiguous*, AWK for *awkward*, RO for *run-on*, etc.), and then hands them back, remarking that everyone needs more work. So immediately it's back to the drills and exercises.

This approach to teaching writing has come to be known as the *product view*. It operates on several assumptions that writing teachers and scholars have come to reject over the last few years. It assumes, for example, that knowing how to spell and punctuate or how to diagram a sentence leads to good writing. Although these skills are important, we should never confuse them with writing performance, nor should we accept the idea that mastering these skills will improve students' writing. Twenty-five years of research demonstrate that grammar instruction does not improve writing skill (see Hillocks, 1986, for a review).

Contemporary work in composition studies suggests that the product view mistakenly emphasizes the end product rather than the process by which students produce that product. Teachers using this approach spend much time telling students what good writing is, but they tend not to provide any means for students to alter their composing behaviors, which is really the only way to improve the finished product.

The *process view* of teaching writing has developed as an alternative to the product view. It focuses on helping students change the way they compose, providing students with situations where language can be used meaningfully, where the emphasis is on the act of writing itself, not finished essays.

As it was initially conceived, the process approach recognizes several stages of composition development. During the planning or prewriting stage, writers generate ideas and begin organizing them. During the writing stage they put these ideas into some rough order. Then, during the revision stage, they polish organization and expression. Finally, during the editing stage, they correct surface errors like spelling, punctuation, and usage.

Perhaps the most important part of the process view is its argument that effective writing instruction focuses on helping students through the composing stages rather than on critiquing the completed essay. Turning classrooms into writing workshops is the means to this end; workshops allow students to share their writing with one another in groups and allow teachers to provide suggestions for improvement as writing takes place. Students develop several drafts of an assignment before turning it in for a grade, and a great deal of time is given to revising papers. Together, these methods result in an emphasis on "process" rather than "product."

We can see that even though the process view of writing instruction addresses "stages" of composing, it also combines the idea that writing is recursive with the idea that it takes place in a social context. It stresses our current awareness that writing is a social action, designed to evoke some response in readers. In this instructional environment, class time is devoted to revising drafts on the basis of feedback provided by teacher and students. Classroom activities consist primarily of writing, talking about the writing, and rewriting.

Going beyond Process

Over the last few years, growing numbers of scholars have argued that the process view of writing instruction does not model the most effective teaching, because it concentrates on the internal processes of individual writers (see Bizzell, 1984; Cooper, 1986; Holzman, 1986; Reither, 1985). The various composing stages, for example, describe individual acts by individual writers, without addressing the place writers occupy as language users in a given community or how that community influences them. To express the social/cultural aspects of literacy, these scholars suggest that a more acceptable model would consider the role society plays in shaping what writers produce.

This amplification of the process view is sometimes referred to as the *pragmatic view* of writing (J.D. Williams, 1989), and it has special significance for bilingual classrooms. Too often our students view writing as an empty exercise. They have not had much reinforcement of the reality that writing is a social action that get things done, such as applying for a job, canceling a subscription, or transmitting information.

The social nature of writing suggests that teachers should strive to give students tasks that allow them to practice functional discourse. Yet most assignments do not meet the need for such reinforcement; most are nonfunctional, simply asking students to describe things, more often than not their personal experiences.

The pragmatic view suggests that teachers concentrate on connecting writing to social, functional tasks that will involve students in a true discourse community. The range of such tasks is varied, of course, but teachers should understand that the idea of language as action indicates that assignments must ask students to produce writing that actually *does* something other than describe or narrate or compare and contrast. Real writers in real discourse communities don't describe something simply for the sake of description; they describe to convey information that readers want or need in one way or another. It is the task of teachers to provide assignments that motivate students to discover a purpose for the writing they do.

Teachers should also be aware that the *form* of the writing they ask young people to do links students to the mainstream social and cultural heritage. When teachers ask students to write a poem, a letter, an essay, or a report, they ask them to draw on the existing conventions for that form, which in many cases students will find quite unfamiliar. Moreover, the very act of using these conventions links writers to a specific social identity that some may not want to accept because it asks them to step outside the parameters of their own communities and their own heritage. Or they may not know how to communicate effectively across cultures, because the act requires a knowledge of both the home culture and the mainstream culture.

To summarize, we would say that at the heart of the pragmatic view is the implication that every writing task be related to the "real world." In practical terms, such tasks will ask students to *do* something in the tangible sense of performing a social action. It also proposes a whole-language approach to teaching, such that reading, speaking, listening, and writing are interrelated activities in the classroom. It has as a major goal helping children see that writing has purpose beyond fulfilling the demands of a school assignment.

CONCLUSION

Issues of literacy affect everything teachers do in the classroom. Every teacher, in one way or another, is a teacher of reading and writing. For language-minority students, literacy seems to take on a special urgency, largely because their achievement in school tends to drop with each year they spend in an English-only curriculum and because many educators believe that their failure is linked to inadequate reading and writing skills.

In most bilingual classes, reading and writing instruction follows a peculiar course: the focus is on surface features, with teachers working hard to get students to pronounce every word correctly or to avoid grammatical patterns in writing that are based on the native language. During reading activities, few pay much attention to developing comprehension skills that involve inferences. During writing activities, few draw on the rhetorical skills students have in their native language to enhance writing tasks in English. In other words, the curriculum focuses on functional literacy skills, rarely expanding to include the social and critical facets of literacy so important to academic achievement and personal fulfillment.

Changing the implicit goal of literacy instruction for bilingual students can be accomplished only through understanding the various factors related to how people read and write. This chapter has outlined some of those factors. Later in the text, we examine some of the ways to develop a classroom environment that applies the ideas discussed above.

CHAPTER 3

Defining Bilingualism

OVERVIEW

Defining bilingualism is a complex task, which explains why linguists, socio-linguists, psychologists, and educators have over the years developed numerous definitions, each one reflecting the particular concern of these specific disci-plines. For the purpose of this book, we begin with a broad definition and elaborate on it as our discussion proceeds. We define bilingualism as *a person's ability to process two languages*.

We begin by examining the process of first- and second-language acquisi-tion, distinguishing among monolinguals and coordinate and compound bilin-guals. We then examine language proficiency and explain what it means in terms of literacy to be proficient in a language for both monolinguals and bilinguals. What emerges is an important distinction between oral proficiency and proficien-cy in academic literacy, the former being simply the ability to communicate in speech and the latter being the more complex ability to comprehend and produce academic discourse. We examine the concepts of context-embedded and context-reduced language in relation to this distinction.

Other concepts are relevant to our discussion of bilingualism, such as communicative competence, language assessment, linguistic interdependence, and transfer. We introduce these concepts as a framework for later arguments.

Numerous factors influence the extent of a person's bilingualism. One of the more powerful is the existing social context. Thus our definition of bilingual-ism will reflect the sociological characteristics that are most visible in legislation governing language policy in education. The chapter concludes with a discussion of some of the measures that have helped shape bilingual programs over the years.

LANGUAGE PROFICIENCY

Language is commonly considered to encompass four skills: listening, speaking, reading, and writing (MacNamara, 1966). When we talk about proficiency in one language we refer to people's ability to process language in each of the four skills. We consider people literate if they are also proficient in reading and writing skills at an appropriate level for a specific context.

When we talk about bilingual proficiency, we refer to the ability to process *two* languages in each of the same four skills. Bilingual proficiency would therefore involve the following: (1) understanding the message in each of the languages spoken, (2) being able to respond in each of the languages in a manner that is appropriate to the situation, (3) being able to read and understand a written message, and (4) being able to write in each language. Each skill may be performed with various levels of competence.

We consider people bilingual if they can process two languages in the first two skills. They are biliterate if they can also read and write in two languages. *The more adept people are at processing the four skills in each of the languages, the greater their level of bilingualism.*

It is important to note that although we have spoken of listening, speaking, reading, and writing skills, we do not mean to imply that each of the skills is separate and unrelated to the other. Nor do we imply that the skills are hierarchically ordered, listening being the lowest and writing the highest on a scale, or that they move in lock-step fashion, such that each level must be mastered before students go on to the next.

As indicated in the previous chapter, we advocate a whole-language approach to literacy instruction that integrates the language modes. We believe that it's possible for students to write even if they lack perfect speaking or reading skills. Reading is possible even if listening skills are underdeveloped, and so on. The language modes interact reciprocally, so the more students read, the more vocabulary they acquire, thereby expanding their speaking repertoire and improving their spelling from seeing words in print. The more students write, the more proficient they become at formulating a clear and concise message, which will in turn positively affect speaking.

Language proficiency is difficult to measure, not only among bilinguals but also among monolinguals, even though a wide range of instruments is currently available for assessment activities (Omaggio, 1986). One that is used extensively in many districts is the Bilingual Inventory of Natural Language (BINL), which measures the oral English language proficiency levels of students whose native language is not English. For certain languages, such as Spanish, it can also be used to measure students' oral proficiency levels in their native language.

The results of the BINL and similar tests are used to determine student placement in a school's language program; they indicate whether students should be placed in an entry-level bilingual program or an English-only program. The results are also used to determine whether a child should exit a bilingual program to participate in an English-only program of instruction. Nevertheless, these tests may provide a distorted picture of students' language skills (see Rosansky, 1981; Ulibarri, Spencer & Rivas, 1980), because they evaluate oral proficiency and may offer no assessment of proficiency in academic literacy.

Academic literacy requires skills and strategies that may not occur frequently in speech, even though the two modes are fundamentally similar. Thus an instrument like the BINL may indicate that students have high oral English proficiency but tell us nothing about their academic discourse skills. Moreover, assessing writing skill is quite controversial even for mainstream students, because the only reliable method, called holistic scoring, may not provide a valid measure of student performance (see White, 1986).

The term "communicative competence" can be especially helpful in understanding language proficiency. It was originally coined by Dell Hymes (1972) to refer to people's pragmatic awareness of what constitutes an appropriate use of language in specific contexts. Communicative competence is related to a wide range of language actions, including assessment. The only way one can begin to determine whether someone is communicatively competent is if the person shows it. Thus a person could be competent in a language, but unless the situation calls for an observable response, no one would ever know. But assessing the degree of communicative competence isn't always a straightforward process, so again teachers are faced with having to select an accurate way to measure competence.

Another facet of communicative competence is the level of language proficiency. For example, one level of proficiency may involve the ability to ask for and understand directions, whereas another may involve the ability to engage in a complex real estate deal. Intuitively, we recognize that it is easier to ask for and comprehend directions in either the native or the second language than it is to conduct a business deal. The latter situation calls not only for an appropriate level of language formality but for correct content and some awareness of business etiquette. (See Canale & Swain, 1980, and Omaggio, 1986, for an in-depth discussion.)

Similarly, the language proficiency required to perform casual classroom routines is not as rigorous as the language proficiency required to understand abstract concepts, which may require extensive background information to grasp fully.

When we speak of language proficiency in the school context, we must distinguish between the level needed for informal, oral communication and the level needed for academic literacy. Cummins (1981a) introduced the concepts "context-embedded" and "context-reduced" language skills to differentiate between school situations that call for the more casual, concrete, experience-based language skills and academic situations that call for literacy-related and abstract skills.

Context-embedded refers to situations that are clear from their context. That is, students can construct meaning on the basis of cues that may be nonverbal. For example, if a teacher holds a book out to a student and utters "Would you like to use this book?" the meaning of the utterance could be determined in most instances on the basis of the action, exclusive of the words that accompany it. Context-reduced, however, refers to situations that require both high-level language proficiency and context knowledge, because the information is abstract and, more important, may not be linked to *nonverbal* cues. When reading, for example, people must rely significantly on the textual cues the writer provides to help construct meaning (see Krashen & Biber, 1988). For this reason, reading and writing are often referred to as "decontextualized" actions (see Hirsch, 1977).

These concepts are important in understanding the behavior of students who attempt to use a second language in school. Although they may seem to get along with native English-speaking classmates and may seem to understand the general classroom routine, teachers must be cautious in ascribing to them a high level of language proficiency. They may not have the level of proficiency or background required to comprehend the more abstract content concepts in textbooks written in English.

FIRST-LANGUAGE ACQUISITION

Language acquisition begins shortly after birth. Halliday (1979) reports, for example, that a one-day-old child will stop crying to attend to his mother's voice. He views this behavior as the first step toward acquisition, as the precursor to actual language. Trevarthen (1974) found that mothers and infants use gestures and body movements to interact with one another, performing a kind of "dance" that involves initiation and turn-taking. He viewed these behaviors as rudimentary forms of communication, the very foundation of speech.

By the age of 18 months, children typically have a vocabulary of only 40 or 50 words, but they combine single-word utterances with gestures and context to communicate a great deal. A few months after their first single-word utterances, they begin combining words into two-word utterances that seem to represent a natural progression toward more complete verbal expressions. Frequently, these appear as "All gone," "Daddy milk," and so forth. Linguists therefore tend to think of language acquisition as a continuum, with children moving from preverbal gestures to single-word expressions, two-word utterances, and finally complete expressions (Clark & Clark, 1977).

Although the source of children's initial utterances is the family, after initial vocabulary building they do not imitate directly the language of those around them. For example, few children are likely to hear the expression "Daddy milk," yet two-year-olds commonly use this utterance to get a glass of milk. The explanation is that English grammar, even among children, can generate an infinite number of meaningful utterances, so most of what young people speak is new, not a repetition of what they hear (see Clark & Clark, 1977; Hudson, 1980; Slobin & Welsh, 1973). Also, when language appears it is related to the baby's immediate environment and directed toward the baby, which explains why we encounter initial utterances like "doggy" and "Daddy," but not "government," "computers," and "mortgage."

This analysis suggests that infants spend the first year or so of life mastering many of the grammatical and pragmatic rules that govern language. Mastery, however, comes from their being part of a language community, not from direct instruction. In this sense, we understand that infants are involved in *acquiring* the language, not *learning* it, because the first is related to unconscious knowledge *of* language and the second is related to conscious knowledge *about* language, which comes when children are older, through formal instruction. Acquired language patterns are internalized and deeply ingrained; many of them last a lifetime. Language learning, on the other hand, is more readily lost over time, unless it is practiced regularly.

Understanding these characteristics of first-language acquisition is important for all teachers, but particularly those involved in helping either monolingual or bilingual students become literate. The reason is that acquired language is predominantly oral, although there is ample evidence that some aspects of literacy are also acquired (Bates, 1979; Calkins, 1983; Dyson, 1982, 1983; Graves, 1979, 1981; Gundlach, 1981, 1982, 1983). Literacy instruction, however, implicitly involves changing oral discourse such that it more closely resembles written discourse.

Because acquired language patterns are so deeply ingrained, they are seldom immediately influenced by direct instruction. This phenomenon puzzles many teachers who may think that literacy instruction proceeds in much the same way as math or history instruction. In history, for example, if teachers want students to know when Columbus reached America, they simply provide the date. If students pay attention, they will later be able to recall "1492." Not much more is required. Formal language instruction, however, is fundamentally different: it asks students to apply consciously learned rules to monitor what essentially is an unconscious, automatic process—their own grammar and lexicon (Farr & Daniels, 1986; Raimes, 1986).

We can demonstrate the difficulty involved with three simple rules we invented for English:

1. All adjectives in English come before nouns, except when the noun is the object of a preposition, in which case the adjective follows the noun.
   Example: The red car revved its engine
   Exception: The car stopped at the light red.
2. All noun subjects in English come before their verbs, except when the noun is preceded by the words "a" or "an," in which case it comes at the end of the sentence.
   Example: The woman asked for directions.
   Exception: A should learn her students' names as quickly as possible teacher.
3. Forms of "be" that function to specify location will always be replaced by the word "zeronome."
   Example: The book zeronome on the table.

We would invite you to study the rules and then to write for 10 minutes, describing what you did over the weekend, applying the rules without error. We've asked many teaching candidates to perform this little test, and the outcome is always the same—most fail to apply the rules accurately; the few who manage to apply them produce either only a handful of sentences or a composition seriously lacking in details, organization, or cohesion, factors not associated per se with the peculiar prose the three rules produce. Learning the rules is easy, but applying them is hard.

In no way are we suggesting that teaching and learning aren't important parts of literacy development. The best teaching will in fact draw on students' acquired language skills to enhance literacy. We do, however, want teachers to understand that literacy instruction tends to proceed slowly, not because teachers aren't prepared or don't spend significant time on task, and not because students aren't trying or capable, but because of the nature of what's involved. Thus, a single lesson on identifying the topics in paragraphs or on English sentence structure is unlikely to transfer to other reading and writing activities. Lessons have to be repeated in different ways many times before learning becomes internalized and influences acquired patterns.

The discussion of literacy in Chapter 1 provides a guide to understanding more clearly what we mean when we say literacy instruction proceeds slowly. Functional literacy is associated with a fourth-grade reading level, implying that many students may need *four years* of instruction to reach minimal proficiency. Cultural literacy and critical literacy, of course, take even longer to develop. This analysis of first-language acquisition, then, suggests teachers must inform their instruction through recognizing that developing literacy is an incremental process that takes time.

SECOND-LANGUAGE ACQUISITION IN CHILDREN

In most instances, second-language acquisition can proceed along the same lines as first-language acquisition (see Gardner, 1980, 1983; Hakuta, 1986; Hatch, 1978; Krashen, 1981a, 1982), although there are some differences. For example, Weinreich (1953) and Ervin and Osgood (1954) distinguish between "compound" and "coordinate" bilinguals to describe two different ways people can become proficient in two languages (Padilla & Liebman, 1982).

A compound bilingual is someone who has acquired two languages at the same time from birth. The two languages may be used interchangeably in a given situation (Ervin-Tripp, 1975), or they may be used separately and only by particular people in particular situations. An example of the latter occurs in Leopold's (1939-1949) study of his daughter. The parents taught her German and English from birth and kept the languages separate: the father spoke in and responded to German only, the mother English only. The child was expected to maintain the language separation and in fact did until she reached late adolescence.

According to Leopold, children who have more than one label with which to identify an object will soon realize that language is an abstraction of reality that can be subjective and malleable. He argues that this realization is responsible for higher cognitive flexibility in bilingual children compared to monolinguals. With labels for each object they experience, children will know that a horse, for example, can be called not only "a horse" but also "un caballo." Rather than being confusing, two labels enhance flexibility and creativity.

A coordinate bilingual is someone who from birth learns to speak in one language first (L_1) and subsequently is exposed to a second (L_2). Hakuta (1986), for example, offers a case study that typifies the process for children who are immersed in an L_2 environment. He describes the acquisition of English by Uguisu, a five-year-old girl whose Japanese parents moved to the United States for two years. Her parents spoke English, but they talked to Uguisu exclusively in Japanese. When Uguisu was enrolled in kindergarten shortly after the family's arrival, she knew no English.

Uguisu continued to speak Japanese for several months, even though she spent her days in an English-language environment. Initially, her English was limited to a few words she picked up from her playmates, such as "I'm the leader." Her teacher didn't know any Japanese and therefore could not provide any formal language instruction, so Uguisu's contact with English was largely informal and consisted of play time with peers. It was similar, in other words, to a child's exposure to his or her first language, except for the lack of parental input.

After seven months in this English environment, Uguisu suddenly began to use English, and it quickly became her dominant language, which means she used it nearly all the time, whether interacting with her parents or playing by herself. Hakuta (1986) reports that "within eighteen months after her initial exposure to English, only a trained ear would have been able to distinguish her for a native speaker" (p. 108). (See Fantini, 1982, for another example of coordinate bilingualism.)

One type of bilingual is not inherently better than the other. Both compound and coordinate bilinguals may or may not develop into "balanced" bilinguals, a term used to describe people who are able to listen, speak, read, and write in both languages with *equal proficiency*. The extent of this ability depends on several factors. One is whether children receive equal experiences in both languages. For example, are they provided with opportunities to listen to stories or songs in both languages? If one language is used exclusively for activities that tend to develop vocabulary, such as listening to and retelling stories, then vocabulary in this language will be more extensive than in the other.

Another factor related to becoming a balanced bilingual is language choice—whether children choose to use one language to the exclusion of the other. Bilinguals often have a language preference (Padilla & Liebman, 1982) that may be based on personal or sentimental reasons, such as the relationships with those who use the particular language in the household. In addition, preference may be based on structural factors that involve society at large.

For example, if one of the two languages spoken is used by one of the parents exclusively to scold the child, it is not likely that a positive feeling may be attached to that language; thus, given a choice, it may not be that child's language of preference. Likewise, if a language is used primarily as the language of intimacy and affection, connected to the person with whom the child has a special relationship, the use of the language may evoke special feelings; thus again, given a choice, it might become that child's preferred language. In short, there are more reasons for bilinguals to choose a certain language than simply linguistic competence.

Outside influences, such as the value attached by mainstream society, can also affect language choice. Some parents may insist that their children speak the prestige language of the mainstream rather than the home language, because they may believe it will lead to increased access to mainstream rewards. Or children may reject the home language because they have chosen to identify with the majority-language mainstream (see Rodriguez, 1982, for an example.)

Finally, there may be very obvious sanctions on the use of the native language in school. For example, Hispanic students in the Southwest have historically been discouraged from using Spanish in school. Or there may be subtle sanctions that indicate to children that their native language is just not as good as the language of the mainstream; therefore, its use is not welcome. Of course, children may still choose their native language, but this choice may not be without some inner conflict. (These and other social issues have had much influence on language-of-instruction policy in school districts across the United States.)

Lambert (1983) coined two terms that succinctly summarize the potential positive or negative aspects of the bilingual experience. When linguistic preference enriches people's language experience and when bilingualism is associated with accomplishments and positive feelings, it is referred to as "additive bilingualism." When bilingualism is associated with feelings of inferiority or punishment, it is referred to as "subtractive bilingualism." Teachers can have a very profound influence on which of these the students experience.

Two important questions arise at this point in our discussion of bilingualism: (1) What is the relationship between the two languages, and (2) how do bilinguals use the two languages? Cummins (1981a) attempts to answer these questions through what he calls the "linguistic interdependence principle," which postulates that both languages have a common rather than a separate base, which he refers to as Common Underlying Proficiency (CUP) (see Cummins & Swain, 1986).

The validity of the interdependence principle is a central assumption in *Literacy and Bilingualism*, and later chapters address it in more detail. At this point, we would suggest that if bilinguals maintain their two languages separately, it would be impossible to use a sentence from one language within the context of the other. It would be impossible to code-switch at will, as bilinguals often do in conversation to make a point, or to use a concept learned in one language to solve a problem in the second language, as bilinguals often do when they use multiplication tables in one language to perform mental mathematical calculations in the other.

LANGUAGE PROFICIENCY AND LITERACY

Cummins' linguistic interdependence principle is particularly significant in a discussion of language proficiency and literacy. Describing a Spanish-English bilingual program, Cummins (1988) notes:

> Spanish instruction that develops Spanish reading and writing skills (for either Spanish L_1 or L_2 speakers) is not just developing Spanish skills, it is also developing a deeper conceptual and linguistic proficiency that is strongly related to the development of literacy in the majority language (English). In other words, although the surface aspects (e.g., pronunciation, fluency, etc.) of different languages are clearly separate, there is an underlying cognitive academic proficiency which is common across languages. This "common" underlying proficiency makes possible the transfer of cognitive/academic or literacy-related skills across languages. (p. 44)

As we mentioned earlier, biliterate bilinguals are able to listen, speak, read, and write in two languages. How well they perform in the two languages determines whether they are balanced bilinguals with equal proficiency in both languages. It also determines what type of input students need to help them become balanced bilinguals.

For example, if children are raised speaking two languages interchangeably, as compound bilinguals, they will be able to speak and listen with equal proficiency in both languages. Yet when they begin attending school, they will probably be taught to read using only one of the two languages, unless a bilingual school is available. The question is: Do these children continue to have equal proficiency in two languages? They have received instruction in one of the two languages, which resulted in their being able to read initially in only one language. How will they become biliterate?

Based on the linguistic interdependence principle, we can say that as children master reading, they will be able to learn to read in the other language as well, without as much effort. They have already acquired some background information on the process and mechanics of reading that they can utilize in reading in the other language. The instruction in reading in one language and connections made by the teacher will thus assist them in future learning. The same can be said for writing.

Let's now take the case of the coordinate bilingual, that is, the child who knows one language from home and is later introduced to another language for the first time in school. This is the case of many immigrants or children of immigrants or of those who temporarily transfer to another country for business reasons or to seek political asylum.

Like monolinguals, coordinate bilinguals will be able to process language skills at various levels of competence, but only in one language at first, not the language of the school. An example would be a five-year-old child who can listen and speak upon arrival at school. He may also possess some prereading and prewriting skills; for instance, he may know the alphabet and may be able to write his name. Another example would be an older child, let's say a nine year old, who may be quite competent in all four of the language skills: listening, speaking, reading, and writing, and might also know content material, such as the capital of some states, some mathematics, some social science. Another example would be an even older child, let's say high school age, who may have superior language skills in one language and in addition know a body of information in content areas, such as science, math, social studies, or literature, depending on academic exposure and level of instruction.

The possibilities and levels of language competence are almost endless and are determined by factors such as age and formal or informal instruction in the four language skills, through school and home. Each of the cases will require differential instruction in the first and second language. Clearly, the instructional needs of a kindergartner who has not acquired the mechanics of reading in any language will be different from the instruction for the fourth-grader who already is literate in one language and who knows the relationship between speech and writing.

The assumption we make here is that each child upon arriving in school has some level of language competence in each, if not all, the four modes we have mentioned—the monolingual child in one language, the bilingual child in two languages. *The fact that children may not speak, understand, or read and write in the language of the school does not mean that they do not speak, understand, or read and write in their home language.* Again, depending on age and experiences, they may be perfectly competent in each of the language skills. They just might not know the language of the school. Therefore, *we cannot assume that such children are linguistically incompetent.*

The question then is: How can children's competence in their native language be used by teachers to foster literacy in the mainstream and in the native language? It is clear at this point that there are two items of utmost importance for teachers: (1) *assessing the home language(s) proficiency level of the child*, and (2) *providing instruction appropriate to the age and native-language proficiency of children through transfer.*

Assessing Students' Language Background and Proficiency Levels

The students who enroll in a school may be compound bilinguals. That is, they learned two languages from birth. Or they may be coordinate bilinguals, who know one language from birth and have later become exposed to the language of the school. Students may or may not be balanced bilinguals, and there are innumerable levels of competency and literacy they may have in either one or both languages.

At one extreme, for example, are students who are bilingual; that is, they speak the language of the school and another language. These students are most likely to learn to read in English and perhaps pursue learning to read in the other language as an enrichment, providing a program is available. At the other extreme are the new arrivals from foreign countries, who are monolingual in a language other than English. Although learning another language will also be enriching, for these students learning to read in English will be a question of necessity, because they must be able to function successfully in school and achieve in the mainstream language.

These two cases are very simple and clear-cut, but they are extreme cases. Between these two extremes we find all the other students with almost infinite combinations of oral competencies and literacy levels in the native language and in the mainstream language. These students will also be of a variety of ages. Not all students who enroll for the first time in American schools are in kindergarten. If they were, things would be considerably simpler.

In reality, students come and go from school regularly, enrolling at different grade levels and ages, from different schools in local areas or other cities and countries. Some of the students will be preliterate, some will be literate. Some will have a working knowledge of English, some will be biliterate, some will have no knowledge of English at all. Assessing the students upon enrollment becomes crucial, because their instructional program will be based on this assessment. An incorrect evaluation of student's skills may cause them either to repeat things they already know in their native language or to be assigned to an inappropriate program where they end up being ignored. In either case, they are likely to suffer an academic setback.

Normally, upon enrollment in a school, students disclose whether they speak a language other than English at home. In Los Angeles, for example, a form called the "Home Language Survey" is used to identify students who may speak other languages. The students' response on this survey triggers other language proficiency and literacy assessment to determine language program placement. Numerous language-assessing instruments are available to measure oral language proficiency, second-language literacy level, and native-language proficiency (see Omaggio, 1986). Between initial school enrollment and language program assignment determination, many decisions have to be made on the basis of assessment results.

Assessment is especially significant for students who started as Limited English Proficient (LEP) in a bilingual program, where they learned to read in the native language. They may have reading skills similar to those of students who are literate in the native language from home instruction or from attending school in their own country, except for the fact that the students who attended bilingual programs in the United States are likely to have higher levels of oral English proficiency. For all of these students, the transferring of skills from the native to the second language is most significant.

Transfer

By transfer we mean *building on what students already know in their native language to teach new skills in the second language*. Although this definition extends from what the concept of transfer usually means in educational psychology, within a bilingual context it has been taken to mean other things.

The reason that transfer is an issue at all in a bilingual program is that it implies the eventual choice of one language over the other. The implication is that it will not be necessary to have instruction in two languages forever and that at some point it will be time to choose one or the other language. In fact, as Fishman (1972) suggested, there is no need to use two languages in identical situations, if one language will suffice.

The word transfer has been used synonymously with the word switch or shift. As it pertains to students who are literate in their native language, transfer has been used to mean the reaching of a certain level in the native language and then immediately switching to the second language, with the same quickness as turning the page of a book. This makes no sense at all pedagogically. Yet, because much research talks about threshold levels above or below which students may do well or poorly, it is possible that this may have contributed to viewing transfer in this fashion.

Transfer is a continuous process of making connections between the native and the second language while students are involved in language-development activities. This is a process that would take place over the entire time that it takes the preliterate student to become literate and the literate student to become biliterate. Students may receive instruction in reading in the native language until they are literate. However, this alone will not prepare them for a curriculum taught in English only. If their English skills are neglected, and no connection is made between native- and second-language skills, transfer will be impossible.

SOCIAL CONTEXT AND BILINGUALISM

Most teachers know that the United States is in the midst of one of the largest waves of immigration in its history. Fleeing poverty, political oppression, or lack of opportunities, millions of Mexicans, Asians, and Central and South Americans are entering the United States to find a better life.

The long-term social consequences of this massive immigration are difficult to specify, but the more immediate effects on our schools are being felt from one end of the nation to the other. Classrooms increasingly are both multicultural and multilingual, and the position English has held in this country since World War I as the dominant, majority language is no longer as secure as it used to be.

Although many Americans find this situation disquieting, we should be aware that the United States is not the only nation facing hard social and educational questions as a result of massive immigration. The last two decades have seen major changes in worldwide demographics as Third World populations have sought a better life in the industrialized countries. England, France, Germany, the Netherlands—each faces numerous social and educational difficulties caused by large-scale immigration.

Bilingual education programs invariably reflect the status of minority languages in a given country, and their goals are related to historical factors, such as the size of the minority-language community, how long it has existed in the country, and its socioeconomic power. For example, in England, France, and the United States, where governments have been forced to deal with large numbers of recent, unskilled immigrants, bilingual programs have tended to focus on replacing the minority language—whether Pakistani, Vietnamese, or Spanish—with the majority language. The goal is monolingualism. In countries like Canada and Sweden, however, we find very different situations; in these countries, large minority-language communities have coexisted with the majority communities for many years. As a result, the goal of educational programs is to foster bilingualism, not to replace the minority language with the majority. Many people in Sweden, for example, view the use of students' first language as a human right (Skutnabb-Kangas 1986).

Differences in the social context for bilingualism seem to influence the effectiveness of bilingual education. We find that immersion programs, wherein students attend classes taught in their second language, have proven quite successful in countries like Canada. Students whose first language is English attend classes in French from grades 6 through 10; students whose first language is French attend classes in English for the same number of years.

Such programs seem to be very successful in achieving the goal of bilingualism in French and English (Genesee, 1987), in part because they establish two majority languages. Immersion programs in the United States, on the other hand, have traditionally focused only on minority-language students and have excluded native English speakers. Thus Spanish speakers may be taught in English, but English speakers are not taught in Spanish, because the goal is English monolingualism not bilingualism. These programs have not been very successful and are often linked to academic failure and high dropout rates among language-minority students.

We need to recognize, however, that even in countries like Canada, socio-historical factors severely limit the scope of bilingualism. Canada has also experienced significant recent immigration, but the government has taken few steps to expand the existing model of bilingualism to accommodate Greek, Hindi, or Vietnamese. Although we find well established English/French programs, we don't find any French/Greek or English/Greek programs (see Genesee, 1987, for two exceptions). Students whose native language is one other than English or French are excluded from the bilingual paradigm and are expected to replace their primary language with one of the existing majority languages.

Legal and Political Issues

Bilingual education in the United States gained official recognition in the 1960s, when the nation's schools began feeling the effects of immigration from Mexico and Latin America. At that time, Florida and the Western border states responded to growing numbers of nonnative English-speaking students by establishing programs in English as a Second Language (ESL) and bilingual education. The aim was to help ease immigrant students classified as LEP into the mainstream. In 1963, the Ford Foundation helped establish a bilingual education program in Dade County, Florida, that taught students in both Spanish and English (Hakuta, 1986).

Prior to this period, language-minority students, particularly Hispanics, had experienced, in some schools, what can only be characterized as language discrimination. They were forbidden to speak Spanish and were subject to punishment if they did. The Civil Rights Movement of the mid-1960s prompted the government to protect language-minority students from such discrimination, and the result was the Bilingual Education Act of 1968. Additional acts followed, as did additional federal funding, with the aim of developing and implementing "new and imaginative elementary and secondary school programs" to meet the needs of LEP students, using "two languages, one of which is English, as medium of instruction" (Federal Register: United States Constitution Public Law 90-247, Sec. 702, 201–205).

It seems clear that the intent of these acts has been to improve the academic performance of LEP students by using their home language and to help them assimilate as rapidly as possible into the English-speaking mainstream. Some educators have criticized this intention, however, arguing that the legislation makes no attempt to maintain the LEP students' linguistic or cultural heritage. Fishman (1981), for example, protests that:

> Under the aegis of the Bilingual Education Act, funds have been provided to state education departments, universities and local school districts for experimental/demonstration programs that temporarily employ non-English mother tongues as co-media of instruction until (hopefully within three years or less), the pupil's English is good enough to become the sole medium of instruction. Thus, the act is basically not an act for bilingualism, but rather, an act against bilingualism. (pp. 517–518)

At issue is the ultimate status of minority languages and the dominance of English. Many scholars argue that government policy and classroom pedagogy should strive for true bilingualism, with all languages having equal status. In this case, the goal of bilingual programs would be to continue to develop students' first language skills while they simultaneously begin learning English. The goal would not be to use the native language as a temporary medium of instruction until it can be replaced with English. Many others argue just the opposite: that if the native language is used at all it must be to a minimal extent. The emphasis should be on English, because a cultural and linguistic hegemony is an unavoidable factor in forging a national identity.

The claims and counterclaims associated with these two positions are many and difficult to unravel. Yet policy and legislation in the United States mandate bilingual programs *without specifying* the role of bilingualism in society at large. The focus of policy has been and continues to be on issues of equity. For example, in *Lau* v. *Nichols*, the Supreme Court declared in 1974 that:

> There is no equality of treatment merely by providing students with the same facilities, textbooks, teachers and curriculum, for students who do not understand English are effectively foreclosed from any meaningful education. (1974, 414 U.S. 563, 94 S.Ct. 786)

Although some educators have interpreted this ruling to imply that the use of students' native language in education may in fact be a right, the decision makes no mention, direct or otherwise, of the role bilingual education is to play in society. Because of this lack of specificity, the argument goes on, and no agreement is in sight.

Educational Obligations

We would note that when a community is confronted with a wave of immigration, the central question is: What is its obligation toward the newcomers? In a participatory democracy like ours, we take it for granted that education is not only a fundamental right of all people but a necessity for the country's survival. Thus it seems reasonable to conclude that the nation is obligated to provide the best education possible to its nonnative English-speaking children.

What constitutes this education is another area of debate, but it is undeniable that, historically, education in all countries and in all times has been the socializing mechanism by which young people are given the tools necessary to participate in the community at large. When the children of immigrants with a low socioeconomic status remain, as a group, in a low-status position after two or three generations, it indicates that something is amiss. Education is their only means of achieving social mobility, and when they fail in significant numbers to become socially mobile, it suggests that the school system is not meeting its obligation. It has failed to teach those skills necessary to move up the social scale.

Many scholars argue that school in fact tends to maintain the inequities of the social system rather than offer avenues of mobility (Apple, 1980; Ogbu & Matute-Bianchi, 1986). Considering that school dropout rates in many states exceed 50 percent among the minority population, it seems that in fact the school is not reaching these people at all, much less making them upwardly mobile.

Yet some language-minority students do succeed. Among immigrant groups, Asians seem to do the best, while Hispanics in the Southwest have the highest dropout rate of all minority groups. Ogbu and Matute-Bianchi (1986), in a study covering a 20-year period, found that Asian students were overwhelmingly represented in college attendance, whereas Mexican-Americans remained underrepresented. The attitude and expectations held for particular immigrant groups seem to make a difference in the achievement of those particular students (Suarez-Orozco, 1987).

We are not suggesting, obviously, that someone set out to prevent certain minority groups from succeeding in school. It is possible, however, that, without anyone being particularly at fault, a situation is created that will not facilitate the success of certain students in school—as when the curriculum asks high school students to use first-grade basal readers because they aren't proficient in English. In this case, and in many others, knowledge of the factors related to literacy and bilingualism can lead teachers to create a positive, success-oriented classroom environment.

We are suggesting that teachers' roles in regard to their students do not change, regardless of how society chooses to meet its obligation to its language minorities: it continues to be educating all students.

This is not an easy task. It demands that teachers be thoughtful and well informed and that they assume a new professional role (Peterson, 1988). Some states are emphasizing this obligation more aggressively than others. California, for example, in its *Model Curriculum Guides and Frameworks* (1985) has established high-level guidelines for every subject and insists they be applied to all students.

CONCLUSION

The complexities of bilingual education often shape what we do in the classroom in subtle ways. For example, society generally doesn't attach much prestige to Spanish, so we may discourage students from using their native language at school, thinking that we are doing them a favor by encouraging them to develop their English skills. We may not consider how our reaction affects students' self-concepts, nor how it reflects a form of linguistic chauvinism that is inappropriate in an educator.

By better understanding what bilingualism is and how educational programs have been developed to address the language needs of students, we are acquiring the foundation we need to create a positive classroom environment for our students, one in which we can provide the best education possible to all the children we work with. The next chapter elaborates on this idea by describing the types of instructional language programs available to students.

CHAPTER 4

Pedagogy: Teaching in More Than One Language

OVERVIEW

This chapter focuses on educational programs that use more than one language for instruction. We discuss the assumptions and goals of the major types of programs, exploring some of the philosophical and political issues that influence how they are structured.

We group the programs into three categories: bilingual education programs, language immersion programs, and other language programs, a category that includes foreign language classes for mainstream English speakers and private tutorials designed to preserve the language and culture of ethnolinguistic minorities.

In many respects, the first two programs reflect the controversial nature of bilingual education in the United States, where society at large is divided about what the country's language policy should be. Should it aim to assimilate non-English speakers into the English-speaking mainstream, reducing first-language proficiency and displacing identification with the native culture? Or should it aim to preserve both native language and culture, complementing them through native-language instruction? Also, who will benefit from these programs? What is gained and what is lost on the personal and social level if one aim is chosen over the other?

And who will pay for these programs? Consider: The majority of our Limited-English-Proficient students are children of unskilled laborers who hold a low status in society. They are usually renters, not home owners, and therefore pay no property taxes, the single largest source of school revenues nationwide.

As a result, they are seen by the majority as making few contributions to the community. Their children are often bused to schools in older neighborhoods where most home owners' children have long since passed the age of compulsory education and who bridle at the idea of subsidizing the education of students who are not part of their community.

Each of these questions can be answered in at least two ways, depending on whether one believes nonnative English speakers should be assimilated into the mainstream or whether one believes the schools should work to preserve both the language and cultural heritage of immigrant groups. The debate continues at such an intense level that many of those involved often lose their objectivity and argue from emotion rather than reason. In the following sections, we outline in greater detail the factors related to this debate and discuss their effects on pedagogy.

BILINGUAL EDUCATION PROGRAMS

Although all bilingual education programs employ English and another language, they can differ in structure and emphasis. Some provide instruction in L_1 in all subject areas until students are literate and proficient in both English and the native language. Others offer instruction in L_1 for content courses and a class in English as a second language; the goal is to shift all instruction to English as soon as students reach a sufficient level of proficiency. We also find programs that use English for instruction in every subject except reading, which is performed in the native language; L_1 reading instruction is discontinued as soon as the child is judged proficient in English.

Underlying these programs is a palpable tension regarding what bilingual education is supposed to achieve. Some educators suggest that our schools should maintain the language and culture of minority students, whereas other suggest that they should help students assimilate into the English-speaking mainstream as quickly as possible. We often find these programs described, therefore, in terms of *transition* and *maintenance*. The two goals are largely incompatible, and as yet there is no consensus regarding which we should strive for. In most districts, the personal ideologies of the teachers and administrators who coordinate the program determine what the instructional focus will be, and currently the majority stress transition rather than maintenance.

Assumptions Underlying Maintenance

The major assumption in a maintenance bilingual education program is that bilingualism is a valuable asset. Language is viewed as encompassing not only communication but heritage, culture, and feelings. As such, maintaining the native language has an affective dimension, that of enhancing language-minority students' self-concepts and pride in their cultural background. It also assumes there are benefits to be found in developing and maintaining minority languages, not only for those who speak them but for the society as a whole.

Generally, proponents of maintenance envision a time when America will be a truly pluralistic society that practices what may be thought of as linguistic egalitarianism (Mackey & Beebe, 1977; Padilla & Liebman, 1982; Ramirez and Castaneda, 1974). A few go further and advocate policies that would actively transform our largely monolingual society into a multilingual one by offering foreign-language instruction to all mainstream English speakers (Cummins, 1988). In this view, multilingualism functions to enrich the quality of life, so native English speakers would have much to gain by mastering another language.

We should note, however, that bilingual education will be enriching only if mainstream society perceives speaking another language to be an asset and if those in the mainstream are eager to learn another language (see Milan, 1982). Theoretically, multilingualism has potential benefits, particularly for LEP students, because minority languages gain status and prestige. Capturing the essence of this view, Fishman (1976) tells us that a policy of multilingualism would give a sense of ethnic legitimacy to the minority-language child and a sense of enrichment to the majority-language child.

Yet on a pragmatic level, the very factors that serve to support the arguments for maintenance programs serve to undermine the notion of multilingual enrichment. Language is indeed important in defining both a personal and a national identity, and it is difficult for most people to avoid feeling a strong sense of linguistic chauvinism regarding the language they grow up with (see Hudson, 1980; Trudgill, 1974). It therefore takes significant pressures, usually socio-economic, to motivate people to master a second language.

We've seen economic pressure at work around the globe since World War II, as the United States has dominated trade and technology. The result has been the remarkable spread of English as the world's *lingua franca* (see McCrum, Cran, & MacNeil, 1986). Outside of communities like Los Angeles, Miami, and San Antonio, socioeconomic pressures for native English speakers to master Spanish or any other language just aren't very strong, so the question of enrichment seems limited to an elitist view of education where a foreign language is as enriching as, say, art or music. This view has yet to find extensive support from America's broad middle class.

Assumptions Underlying Transition

Those programs that emphasize shifting from the native language to English assume that language is the single most important factor in fostering a national identity and that widespread, official use of other languages will undermine social unity (Heath, 1983). They also assume that replacing minority students' native language with English will offer socioeconomic mobility and allow students to assimilate into the cultural mainstream.

The emphasis, therefore, is on a quick transition from the category of limited English proficient to English proficient. Proponents recognize both the need for and the benefits of initial native-language instruction, but they often express concern over the possibility that students may spend too much time receiving instruction in their native language, which they assume will result in students' falling behind English-speaking students in their age group.

Although these assumptions accurately reflect our present knowledge of sociolinguistic realities (Baugh, 1984; Gumperz, 1982; Hall, 1972; Harder, 1984; Haugen, 1966; Holzman, 1986; Hudson, 1980; Levinson, 1983; Trudgill, 1974), critics of transition programs argue that they have been used to veil discriminatory language policy decisions. Leibowitz (1976), for example, claims that transition programs have been "coupled with discrimatory legislation and practices . . . , including private indignities of various kinds which made clear that the issue [of bilingual education] was a broader one" (p. 450). Other critics charge that transition programs, in replacing native languages and displacing native cultures, function as a means of social control, because they produce high numbers of dropouts who go on to fill the lower rungs of the socioeconomic ladder (Amastae, 1981; Garcia, 1983; Griswold del Castillo, 1984). In other words, they indirectly provide a large pool of cheap labor for jobs that other members of society refuse to take.

Bilingual Education as Compensatory

During the 1960s, a whole new body of data on language became available as various researchers studied the relationship between literacy and cognition (a topic we discuss in greater detail in Chapter 5). Although the focus of these data was to evaluate cognitive functioning among nonliterate and often non-schooled people, many scholars interpreted them as being applicable to certain minority populations in the United States, and they used the findings as a basis for making recommendations concerning language policy (see Epstein, 1978; Ong, 1978, 1982; J. D. Williams, 1989).

The research involved comparative studies between literate and nonliterate subjects, and the results suggested that sophisticated cognitive skills, such as the ability to reason abstractly, are related to literacy skills: the literate subjects in the studies could perform cognitive tasks that the nonliterate subjects couldn't. When these findings were applied to school-age populations in the United States, particularly blacks and immigrant Hispanics, the conclusion was that children from primarily oral backgrounds, children who had had few opportunities to read, were deficient in terms of language and literacy. This deficiency supposedly translated into cognitive deficiencies.

Although both the research and the notion of cognitive deficiencies have been repudiated among psychologists and linguists since the early 1970s, they are quite resilient and are widely accepted in, among other places, composition studies (see Dillon, 1981; Ong, 1978, 1982; Rose, 1988; Shaughnessy, 1977). But they have also had a significant effect on legislation governing bilingual education, because lawmakers have been influenced by academics who, with the best of intentions, shaped a language policy two decades ago using a fundamentally flawed model of the relationship between mind and language (see J. D. Williams, 1989).

The result has been that, until recently, legislated policies have generally fostered a compensatory view of bilingual education, with the underlying assumption being that students whose native language is not English are linguistically deprived. As a result, the focus in many programs has been on remediating the "language deficiency of linguistic minorities" (U.S. Department of Health, Education, and Welfare Memorandum, 1970). Critics argue that such programs reveal the mainstreams' condescending attitude toward the culture of language minorities and that they also impose fiscal hardship on school districts. Attitude and hardship combine to eradicate students' native language (see Milan, 1982).

LANGUAGE TRANSFERABILITY THEORY

The literature on bilingual education has often been characterized by contradictory findings. Cummins (1981a) argues that abandoning the language-deficit model will eliminate such contradictory results. The underlying assumption in early work was that proficiency in the native language was separate from proficiency in the second language. Cummins refers to this as the Separate Underlying Proficiency model (SUP). According to the SUP model, achievement in the second language was unrelated to the native language and was based solely on second-language exposure, leading to the belief that the prescription of more instruction in the second language would resolve the limited-English problem. To replace the SUP model, Cummins suggests that languages have a Common Underlying Proficiency (CUP). Bilinguals express their language proficiency in two modes, the native and the second language. Thus, the concepts known in one language are transferable to the other. When concepts are learned in the stronger language, they can later be expressed in the second language, not necessitating relearning.

The CUP model suggests linguistic interdependence between languages, and several studies support this hypothesis. Among the ones more cited are the Rock Point Navajo Project (1971), the Sante Fe Bilingual Project (1978), the Nestor School Bilingual Program Evaluation (1978), and the Legaretta study (1979) (see California State Department of Education, 1981). In addition, much research has shown that older students who have highly developed native-language skills tend to acquire cognitive skills in the second language more rapidly than students with less developed native-language skills (Ekstand, 1977;

Genesee, 1978; Krashen, 1978), lending additional support to the idea of language transferability. Toukomaa and Skutnabb-Kangas (1977) found that proficient bilinguals who had attained the highest threshold level of bilingual proficiency showed positive cognitive effects; limited bilinguals, weak in both native and second language, showed negative cognitive effects.

Cummins further hypothesized that language proficiency can be classified into Cognitive Academic Language Proficiency (CALP) and Basic Interpersonal Communicative Skills (BICS). He defines CALP as the higher-level language skills required for literacy and for cognitively demanding content; BICS is the conversational proficiency level often achieved in beginning ESL classes. Quick-exit proponents, according to Cummins, use the BICS level of English proficiency as the exit criterion rather than the CALP, even though the latter may be a better predictor of success in all-English programs. Furthermore, they assume a CUP model in early years, by beginning reading instruction in the native language, but revert to a SUP model when they attempt to mainstream LEP students as soon as possible into all-English programs.

Proponents of late bilingual education exit and of a strong literacy foundation in the native language argue in favor of native-language development until the later elementary years to ensure a successful transfer of high-level cognitive skills to a second language (Cummins, 1981b; Legaretta-Marraida, 1981). Proponents of quick-exit, represented by much of the legislative body in the United States, argue in favor of mainstreaming LEP students as quickly as possible into the English-medium curriculum. To proponents of quick exit, the late reclassification of LEP students may seem in fact like a maintenance bilingual program, because the students will continue to develop their mother tongue to a "high" cognitive level before switching to the second language. Conversely, as Cummins (1979) points out, to late-exit advocates, the early exit may seem akin to reverting to the old "submersion" model in dealing with language minorities (see "Immersion Programs" later in this chapter).

Reclassifying Students

When the focus of a bilingual program is on transition, procedures for reclassifying students as English proficient are very important. At some point students require an evaluation that assesses their readiness for the traditional English-only curriculum.

Most states have established specific reclassification criteria (also known as exit criteria) for LEP students, and they are a constant source of controversy, owing to the differing views on bilingual education discussed above. These differences notwithstanding, teachers and administrators involved in reclassifying students characteristically must address four major questions that are at the heart of the process:

1. How much time should a student spend in a bilingual program to receive the maximum benefits offered by native-language instruction?
2. What is the optimal point for assessing proficiency?
3. What instruments should be used?
4. What criteria can best predict future success in English-only programs?

For many people outside bilingual education, these questions often appear to have straightforward answers that lie in pedagogy and teacher evaluations. The situation in most districts, however, is hardly ever that simple. Several factors strongly affect reclassification decisions, and many of them are beyond the control of individual teachers.

For example, funding nearly always plays a significant role in the application of exit criteria. The cost of providing bilingual instruction can mount rapidly in schools where the majority of the students are nonnative English speakers. Finding qualified bilingual teachers is extremely problematic, so districts will have to hire aides who function primarily as interpreters to assist teachers. In addition, they must also provide teaching materials written in students' native languages, materials for ESL instruction, and staff development programs to train teachers, aides, and administrators in how best to work with language-minority children. These fiscal problems, coupled with philosophical beliefs that favor rapid transition, create administrative pressures to reclassify students as quickly as possible.

Teachers, especially those who are newly credentialed, often feel powerless in the face of administrative urging for rapid exit. As a result, most LEP students are reclassified within one year, some within as little as four or five months, even though linguistic research uniformly shows that it generally takes about 18 months to develop fluent conversational skills. Literacy skills, of course, take much longer to develop.

Rapid reclassification is not an explicit part of any district's official policy, of course, but too often the guidelines, although clear, are simply not adhered to. Those who implement them often stress, consciously or unconsciously, the superficial aspects of exit criteria, giving students and parents a false expectation of future success in English. Emphasizing English proficiency, without a balance of corresponding L_1 proficiency, leads to English instruction in *general* language skills rather than more specific (and academic) *literacy* skills. The result is a superficial mastery of English that dooms most bilingual students to academic failure once they are asked in English-only classes to read (for comprehension, not just decoding or pronouncing the words), write, and develop content knowledge (Snipper, 1985).

Finally, rapid reclassification is commonly influenced by another factor: teachers' frustration at being unable to provide an appropriate instructional program in students' native language. Many teachers, for example, overcompensate for their lack of training in bilingual education by intensifying English reading instruction, which may help students meet minimal reclassification criteria but does little to increase their real achievement (Snipper, 1985).

IMMERSION PROGRAMS

Immersion education in its fundamental form provides dual instruction in L_1 and L_2 over a period of years, until students are proficient in both languages. It does not, as is commonly believed, preclude use of the native language. Like bilingual education, the goal of immersion may be bilingualism or monolingualism.

In the United States, there have been two types of immersion programs. One is directed toward mainstream English-speaking students and has bilingualism as its goal. An example of such a program is the Culver City Project in California, which provides content-area instruction in Spanish to native English speakers. The other type is directed toward language minorities and has English monolingualism as its goal. Language-minority students in such a program receive content-area instruction in English; given the social difficulties associated with being a minority student in a language-majority classroom, this type of immersion is commonly known as "submersion."

In terms of educating language-minority children, the operational rationale for immersion is improved academic performance in English. The goal is to give such students the general language skills and the specific academic literacy skills they need to compete with native English-speaking children. The goal has rarely been realized, however, because it is linked to the broader goal of English monolingualism. This broader goal fails to recognize the importance of native-language skills in developing second-language proficiency. In attempting to eradicate the native language, language-minority immersion programs destroy the very foundation of students' eventual academic success in English. That is, the goals of improved academic performance in English and English monolingualism are incompatible.

Several studies have examined the academic performance of children in immersion programs, and they suggest majority-language children fare better than minority-language children (California State Department of Education, 1984; Phillipson & Skutnabb-Kangas, 1986). Both the St. Lambert Experiment in Canada and the Culver City Immersion Project in California have shown positive results in native- and second-language academic achievement with mainstream, English-speaking children who were immersed in French in the first case and Spanish in the second. Other immersion programs in German, Spanish, and French for mainstream native English speakers in the United States report similar results (see Montgomery County Public Schools, 1976; Samuels & Griffore, 1979).

Lambert (1983) argues that these findings are consistent with his view that immersion for majority students constitutes additive bilingualism. He maintains that these students can surpass the achievement of nonparticipating peers in their native language, while enjoying the benefits of the enrichment provided by the second language. He further argues that immersion for language-minority students constitutes subtractive bilingualism, because the programs are not specifically designed for them and are in fact harmful to children's identities and social development. Cummins (1980) suggests that prestige, a positive self-concept, and society's support for the dominant language facilitate the success of L_2 immersion for majority children.

Not all studies, however, have shown positive results for majority students. Modiano (1968), working in Chiapas, Mexico, found that immersion reduced students' academic achievement levels (see Skutnabb-Kangas, 1984, for a review of other studies). In addition, MacNamara (1966), after evaluating immersion education in Ireland, reported negative effects on the cognitive development of bilingual students. He concludes that "a bilingual pays for his L_2 skills by a decrease in L_1 skills. . . . There is a balance effect in language learning at least where the time devoted to the second language is so extensive that the time available for the mother tongue is reduced" (p. 136).

Although MacNamara's conclusions may seem to reflect simple common sense, we see in Chapter 5 that any attempt to establish a causal relationship between language and cognition should be highly suspect. Moreover, in the context of the classroom, his conclusions are often seen as a means of validating instruction. Some educators, for example, use them to argue against reading instruction in L_1 and English, claiming that reading skills in both languages suffer as a result (see Trites, 1976). They have also been used to argue that a mismatch between the language used in school and the language used at home will result in poor academic performance (see Downing, 1974).

These mixed results for immersion programs certainly suggest that additional research is needed to clarify the roles native-language and second-language instruction play in the long-term academic achievement of language-minority students. They also seem to indicate that language alone may not be the principal factor affecting academic performance. Given the psychosocial nature of language, we shouldn't be surprised by this perception. Moreover, a large body of research indicates that such factors as family and teacher expectations significantly affect student achievement (see Graves, 1981; Gundlach, 1981, 1982; Harste, Burke & Woodward, 1983; Heath, 1983). Perl and Wilson (1986), for example, after studying student writers for four years, conclude that the major factor governing classroom writing performance is teacher expectations.

If this analysis is accurate, and the studies cited above suggest it is, our schools and teachers themselves may unwittingly contribute to low academic achievement among language-minority students. The students' difficulties with Standard English cause even the most sensitive, well-meaning teachers to expect them to have more problems with reading and writing than their mainstream counterparts.

The fact that language-minority students generally do have greater difficulties reinforces teacher expectations to such a degree that a teacher may not recognize par performance when it occurs, causing striving students to grow frustrated and apathetic. Furthermore, language serves the important function of allowing people to define themselves in relationship to others. In the case of language-minority students, their language use seems to define them as low achievers among teachers, administrators, mainstream peers, and society at large. Thus low expectations may become a self-fulfilling prophecy that prevents them from reaching above a certain level of achievement.

SOCIOLINGUISTIC ISSUES AND PEDAGOGY

The fact that language-immersion programs have been successful with some majority-language students and with certain minorities lends support to the vast body of social research advocating that issues of a broader social nature intervene in creating an ambience where the school can or cannot be successful. Michael Apple (1980), for example, talks about a "hidden curriculum" in the nation's schools. He argues that this curriculum underlies what is taught to students and that it works to maintain minorities, who may or may not be non-English speakers, at a low level of achievement. Students learn subject matter while at the same time they learn that they are not going to be able to achieve at the same rate as students in the mainstream. Along the same lines, Carnoy (1974) argues that the mainstream engages in "cultural imperialism" to keep minorities at a low level of achievement. Ogbu (1983) analyzes class relations in terms of caste and talks about the "ceiling effect" as a level above which certain minorities cannot rise.

Such arguments are based on a common assumption: the existence of an underclass of individuals whose underachievement in school is unavoidable as long as the same societal relationships are maintained. Unfortunately, rather than offering solutions, these arguments leave educators with a dilemma. If, in fact, underachievement in school is unavoidable for ethnic and linguistic minorities, given the status quo, why bother looking for effective strategies and programs? If socioeconomic status is such a powerful determinant of school success, it would be reasonable to conclude that children who would have done well in school will continue to do well regardless of the quality of their curriculum and the teaching they receive. Those who would not do well because of low socioeconomic status will continue to fail as predicted, owing to a combination of self-fulfilling prophecy and lowered teacher expectations. In both cases, the school makes no difference in the education of either low- or high-socioeconomic-status students.

Although we recognize that language is not the sole factor that will make a student succeed or fail, as dedicated educators we want a solution to the dilemma. Therefore, we recommend adopting an educational approach that capitalizes on the positive. That is, the ultimate goal of a language program should be "additive," aiming at building on students' native language rather than at eradicating it. Our assumption is that academic achievement can increase for all students, not only the mainstream, if schools change the way the curriculum is delivered, applying the broad goal of bilingualism rather than monolingualism and being aware of student proficiencies.

On this account, we would suggest that second-language immersion programs can be successful for all students, not just those of the mainstream, if they are properly and systematically administered and if bilingualism is the goal. It is possible that the success of immersion programs for some majority students has little to do with the students but very much to do with the fact that the programs have been systematically implemented by a well-trained staff in an educationally sound manner. Moreover, they have not tried to supplant the students' native language.

The Culver City Project, for example, in existence since 1972, has been quite successful. The students are native English speakers whose parents are actively involved in the school. Powerful parent involvement ensures that an appropriate instructional program is delivered by appropriate personnel in an appropriate way.

The program was originally designed after the St. Lambert Experiment in Canada, with bilingualism as the ultimate goal. This is significant. Although the students were taught in the second language beginning in kindergarten and first grade, they also received systematic reading instruction in English, which gradually increased until it was balanced (50% English/50% Spanish) with Spanish by the sixth grade. A native-language component exists and is a significant part of the immersion education.

This type of immersion program is quite different from the submersion that many linguistic minorities have received, where the curriculum is meant for native English speakers (Genesee, 1987) or where it is at best a haphazardly implemented bilingual program (Snipper, 1985) with monolingualism in English as the final goal. We are not advocating that all minority language students be taught through an immersion program, although that is certainly an alternative. But certainly we believe that any program can be successful if it uses an appropriate methodology and if it is systematically implemented.

Many bilingual programs are not always implemented according to policy (Snipper, 1985), but when they are properly implemented they lead to higher academic achievement (Willig, 1985). Whether second-language immersion or bilingual programs are used with LEP students, it is very important that both languages be developed. Recent research with Turkish children in Germany (Rehbein, 1982, 1984) shows that there is a developmental interrelationship between the two languages children are learning and that concepts in content matter and discourse skills the child possesses in the native language are transferred to the second.

Rehbein (1984) found that the ability of children to comprehend complex school textbooks in German was related to their ability to comprehend them in Turkish. He concludes that the degree of development in conceptual information in the second language is related to the degree of coordination achieved in developing both languages (McLaughlin, 1986). It therefore seems that each language-learning system complements the other and that the two languages interact to mutual advantage.

Given such findings, we would suggest that teachers should work to capitalize on the interaction between students' native language and English. The concept that one language helps the other can extend also to the cultural elements that each individual possesses. Cultural values and beliefs will also aid one in understanding and adopting the second culture's set of norms and rules. The native-language skills, we believe, as well as the native cultural values transmitted in the home, are certainly not detrimental to new learning. They can only provide greater insights to a person who is about to become bilingual, and a baseline on which to attach new learning.

OTHER LANGUAGE PROGRAMS

A language program that is not widely implemented but that holds much promise for bilingual education is an XSL (the X representing a second or foreign language) component within a traditional bilingual program. Traditional programs have two major elements: (1) instruction in the native language, and (2) instruction in English, or ESL. With an XSL component, mainstream students would be able to participate in learning a second language as a regular part the total curriculum. In the early 1970s, schools that received Title VII funds from the federal government tended to implement this component. Currently, the San Diego Bilingual Demonstration Project and the Eastman Project in California are among the few such programs.

Foreign-language programs occur most frequently in secondary schools and colleges and are designed to teach native English speakers Spanish, French, German, Russian, and so on. These programs are very different from ESL classes for language minority students. In addition to the oral communication component, they have a reading and writing component that develops cultural awareness as well as literacy in the language. The foreign language is analyzed and explained in English, providing students with a useful level of metalinguistic awareness.

A related category of classes exists as weekend and after-school tutorials, the goal of which is to maintain the native language of immigrant children. In Los Angeles, for example, large numbers of Japanese parents have their children enrolled in after-school tutorials, in many cases because they are residing in the United States only for a short time and will be transferred back to Japan after a few years. In San Francisco, the Chinese community has for decades provided weekend language classes designed to preserve both the language and the culture of mainland China.

Such classes fit the category of enrichment bilingual-education programs, even though we often don't identify programs outside the school day as being part of children's education. These sorts of classes rarely come under attack as other bilingual education programs do. The benefits they provide are seldom challenged. One rarely hears that children are doing poorly in school because they are learning Japanese on weekends. The enriching and additive nature of these classes is generally taken for granted. There are essentially two reasons for this lack of criticism. First, these programs aren't paid for out of public funds. Second, they don't impinge upon the traditional school curriculum, so they don't require teachers to engage in any special preparation.

CONCLUSION

The difficulties teachers face when working with language-minority students are very real, and they go far beyond the day-to-day problems inherent in trying to teach students who aren't proficient in English. In essence, a teacher's job is made more demanding by nonpedagogical issues and conflicting goals related to implementing bilingual education.

As members of American society and as torchbearers for American culture, teachers may feel compelled to adopt the view that language-minority students should be mainstreamed as quickly as possible. They may also occasionally resent the funds that go to bilingual programs when they perceive that this money theoretically could go toward enhancing the traditional curriculum.

It seems clear, however, that more is involved in educating language-minority students than providing drills and exercises related to English grammar or reclassifying them into English-only classes as quickly as possible. It may take years for language-minority children to become literate in academic English. No one's interests are served if they are reclassified too early, for their ultimate personal failure is also a social, an institutional, and a professional one. The situation calls for a reevaluation of what successful instruction should be.

CHAPTER 5

Meeting the Needs
of Individual Students

OVERVIEW

This chapter begins with an analysis of bilingualism and intelligence, summarizing a range of studies that present conflicting data on the intellectual abilities of bilinguals. Based on what we currently know about the nature of mind and language, such studies are bound to produce mixed results because they mistakenly assume a causal relationship between intelligence and bilingualism. No such relationship exists, so the research findings apparently reflect little more than the individual mental abilities of the subjects involved and are not generalizable.

We continue with a discussion of cognitive development to provide a framework for what we do in the classroom. The question of the relationship between mind and language is explored in detail, with particular attention given to the idea that language and literacy influence cognition. Although in bilingual education it is widely believed that language does in fact influence cognitive processes, close examination reveals that such is not the case. There may be a reciprocal relationship between mind and language, but it does not appear to be causal.

The chapter concludes with a framework for teaching strategies aiming at biliteracy. This framework consists of three student categories—preliterate, literate, and postliterate—we use to propose specific pedagogical techniques.

Within a bilingual context, each of these categories refers to the students' native language. Our assumption here is that the concept of literacy applies to whatever language students are able to read and write in. If students are literate in their native language but not in the mainstream language, they are considered literate; if they are literate in their native language as well as in the mainstream language, then we are speaking not of literacy but of biliteracy.

BILINGUALISM AND INTELLIGENCE

Part of the difficulty teachers face when working with nonnative English speakers arises out of the human inclination to judge people's intelligence by how they use the language. The context of academic literacy intensifies this inclination whenever students are asked to write, because, in school, intelligence is often explicitly linked to language skill (see Farr & Daniels, 1986; Hudson, 1980; Trudgill, 1974).

Admittedly, it isn't easy to avoid equating intelligence with language skill; language is one of many cues that we use to identify others and to evaluate or assign their social status. We engage in this evaluation with everyone, not just with nonnative English speakers. For example, people born and raised on the West Coast have a certain view of people who speak with a New York accent, and vice versa.

Nevertheless, when working with nonnative speakers, we can increase our sensitivity to the difficulty they face by considering how hard it would be for us to go to school in Korea or China or Mexico with only a modest knowledge of the native language. You may be a brilliant student, but a poor command of, say, Chinese would make you seem awkward, stumbling, and generally not very bright in front of a class.

Recognizing that we can't really equate intelligence with the ability to use a foreign language is an important first step toward effective instruction. After all, believing that language-minority students are unintelligent because they cannot speak or write flawless English inhibits the educational process. Teachers who hold this view will have lower expectations of their students, and, because of the peculiar self-fulfilling dynamic that exists between teacher expectations and student achievement, these students will indeed perform at a low level.

A range of evidence supports this conclusion, such as Perl and Wilson's (1986) important work. After studying writing classes for four years, they found that teacher expectations and attitudes toward students most clearly distinguished successful instructors from unsuccessful ones. The teachers who helped their students achieve the largest gains in writing performance were those who treated students as people with considerable linguistic and rhetorical knowledge and who had very high expectations of individual achievement. The unsuccessful teachers, on the other hand, not only tended to view students as being linguistically deficient but as being empty vessels waiting to be filled. Perl and Wilson (1986) report that in classrooms where this latter view was evident, even the soundest instructional methods failed to produce significant gains in performance.

We must recognize, however, that numerous studies suggest that bilingualism is inherently "bad" because it leads to a form of intellectual confusion, where children become handicapped in both their first language and their second. The tendency of bilingual children to mix vocabularies, using words and expressions from both languages in their speech, is often pointed to as evidence of such confusion. In addition, many investigations of bilingualism and intellectual performance have shown that monolinguals consistently outperformed bilinguals on language tasks as well as intelligence tests (see Anastasi, 1980; Christiansen & Livermore, 1970; Killian, 1971; M. Smith, 1939; Yoshioka, 1929).

Killian (1971), for example, administered a battery of tests to compare intelligence and language abilities among English monolinguals, Spanish monolinguals, and English/Spanish bilinguals. The bilinguals performed significantly lower on both measures than did the monolinguals.

In another study, Anastasi and Cordova (1953) evaluated Spanish/English bilinguals from Puerto Rico. Thinking that the language used in presenting tests to bilingual subjects might influence results, these researchers gave one administration in Spanish, a second in English. Yet the language of administration seemed to make no difference in the results: the subjects performed well below the norms for monolingual subjects in both test conditions.

The researchers conclude that bilingualism was a major factor involved in the poor test performance:

> [Bilingualism] makes them deficient in both languages. . . . In so far as this maladjustment itself appears to have arisen from the children's severe language handicap during their initial school experiences, a solution of the language problem would seem to be a necessary first step for the effective education of migrant Puerto Rican children. (p. 17)

For various reasons over the last several years, many researchers have severely criticized studies that suggest intellectual and cognitive deficits in bilingual children (see Peal & Lambert, 1962; Swain & Cummins, 1979). Peal and Lambert (1962), for example, after a close analysis of many early investigations, determined that researchers who found monolinguals outperformed bilinguals were actually testing dissimilar groups. The bilinguals were not balanced bilinguals, proficient in both languages. Their lack of fluency had a negative effect on their ability to use L_2 effectively, thus resulting in lower performance scores. When researchers ensured that similar groups were being compared, the bilinguals performed just as well as the monolinguals, and in some cases performed better (see Bruck, Lambert & Tucker, 1974; Cummins, 1976; Duncan & De Avila, 1979; Lambert, 1977, 1978a).

Other investigators have argued that the performance differences are the result of using subjects from dissimilar socioeconomic groups, with the monolinguals coming from the middle class and the bilinguals from the lower class (see Christiansen & Livermore, 1970; Garcia, 1983). Socioeconomic status, of course, has consistently been related to IQ scores; people at the lower end of the scale tend to have lower scores than those at the higher end.

These conflicting results are vexing because as teachers we often feel the need for clear-cut answers to questions about how our students learn and achieve.

Parents who speak a language other than English at home are likely to be concerned about the effects of bilingualism, and if they ask a teacher how two languages may affect school performance and achievement, they won't be satisfied when they hear that the evidence is inconclusive.

In *Mirror of Language*, Kenji Hakuta (1986) takes a significant step toward explaining the problem when he notes that the majority of the negative findings on bilingualism and intelligence have come from the United States, where bilingualism has historically been linked to racial and ethnic groups on the periphery of mainstream America. The positive findings, on the other hand, have generally come from Canada, which has a long tradition of French/English bilingualism, with the French-speaking community a vital social force in Quebec Province.

He suggests that the equivocal results may reflect different sociopolitical climates. In the United States, researchers have interpreted data in a context that stressed *looking for* negative findings; in Canada the opposite is true—the context stressed looking for positive findings.

Although scholars have long understood that social context influences the interpretation of data, more seems to be at work here than this simple explanation can account for. Measuring the degree of a person's bilingualism may be problematic, but assessing an IQ test isn't, especially in view of the nonverbal, culture-fair tests that were developing during the 1960s to avoid language/culture biases. Tabulating scores is a straightforward quantitative process that doesn't readily lend itself to being influenced by social context. The score is either high, or it isn't, and the test-takers are either bilingual (to one degree or another) or they aren't.

Implicitly recognizing the difficulty in attempting to explain the mixed results on the basis of social context, Hakuta (1986) hypothesizes that previous investigators may have committed a fundamental error in trying to compare inherently dissimilar groups, monolinguals and bilinguals, which he believes would lead to distorted results.

In an effort to test this hypothesis, Hakuta and Diaz (1984) and Hakuta (1984) evaluated intelligence and linguistic skills in 300 bilingual Puerto Rican children without comparing them to monolinguals. In both studies, the researchers operated under the premise that bilingualism is a performance continuum, with some individuals being more bilingual than others. Thus, if bilingualism affects cognitive ability and overall linguistic performance, it should be possible to evaluate these variables *within* a group of bilingual subjects without reference to a monolingual group. The investigation evaluated subjects' level of bilingualism, their intelligence, and their degree of language awareness. Values were then correlated to determine how the variables interacted.

The results were disappointing. They showed a modest, but nonsignificant, correlation between intelligence and bilingualism and no correlation at all between bilingualism and language awareness. In other words, the results were just as inconclusive as those we have already examined.

We would argue that, from a psychological perspective, there is no reason at all to predict a relationship between bilingualism and intelligence. A cause-effect relationship simply does not exist; that is, bilingualism is not a causal factor in intelligence. All other things being equal, the bilingual children in the studies above who scored low on IQ tests probably would have achieved the same score had they been monolingual. After considering the lack of a causal relationship, Hakuta (1986) concludes that "bilingualism . . . bears little relationship to performance on these measures [intelligence and linguistic performance]" (p. 40).

Given the difficulties involved in mastering another language, we should view even modest successes as important accomplishments. Certainly, we can't ignore the errors our students produce when they read and write English, but we can and should see those errors as being necessary to acquiring literacy. In fact, careful analysis shows that most of the syntax and vocabulary problems we find in bilingual writing fall into categories of error that are closely related to the level of developing competence in English, not to intelligence (see Edelsky, 1986; Farr & Daniels, 1986). Beneath those surface problems one often discovers a thoughtful composition. As students gain greater competence (and confidence), the number of errors will decrease.

COGNITIVE DEVELOPMENT

Although the absence of any causal relationship between bilingualism and intelligence suggests that investigations in this area may be misdirected, we recognize that the question serves as a preface for a much broader and ultimately more important topic, the relationship between mind and language.

Our understanding of mind and language has been greatly influenced by Jean Piaget and Lev Vygotsky, psychologists whose work with children in the 1920s and 1930s defines the roles cognition and language play in personal development. In some respects their views overlap, but on the whole they are fundamentally dissimilar. (Let us note that in the following discussion we use "cognition" in two ways: the first is very broad and is related to information processing; the second is narrower, related to cognitive capacity.)

We examine their views in some detail below, but at this point we can anticipate the discussion by noting the following: Piaget suggests that cognitive abilities developmentally precede linguistic abilities, so they are necessary for the development of linguistic structures (see Trimbur, 1987). That is, cognition influences language. Vygotsky (1962), on the other hand, suggests that language precedes and significantly influences cognition (also see Whorf, 1956).

Vygotsky's view has become increasingly popular over the last dozen years, in part because he emphasizes the idea that language develops in a social context. His work therefore provides a powerful and potentially valuable theoretical framework for teachers and scholars who perceive language as a social action intimately linked to particular discourse communities.

A related aspect of this social view has emerged and gained strength in composition studies, where numerous educators, citing Vygotsky, maintain that written discourse is inherently superior to oral discourse because it represents an evolution in terms of form and content. The chief advocates, writers like Dillon (1981), Hirsch (1977), Moffett (1985), and Ong (1978) argue that written discourse is linked to the ability to reason abstractly and that without literacy, people are limited to concrete, situational thinking. Let's examine these two views in greater detail.

Does Cognition Influence Language?

A basic principle in all discussions of language acquisition is the notion that language is innate. Any healthy child in a normal environment will develop language just as surely as he or she will walk, because we are genetically predisposed to use language.

The lack of choice in this regard is important, because it suggests that language operates to a significant degree through autonomous mechanisms that are outside the cognitive domain. It follows, therefore, that a great deal of what we do with language, especially at the level of grammar, is beyond conscious control and operates more or less automatically. Jerry Fodor (1983), in fact, suggests that language processes—such as judging the grammaticality of a sentence, parsing sentences into their component parts, and comprehension—are essentially *reflexes*.

Many people who study and teach reading and writing are understandably uncomfortable with this idea. Writing instruction, for example, presupposes not only that writers make conscious decisions when they construct prose but that readers make equally conscious decisions when they construct meaning. Moreover, to propose that composing involves something as unsophisticated as a reflex attenuates the artistic dimension of writing that most teachers hold dear. Given these factors, we can see the appeal of the idea that cognition influences language: it negates the innateness position by keeping language inside the domain of cognition.

We find the basis for this position in Piaget's (1953, 1955, 1962, 1974) model of children's intellectual development. He suggests that children go through a continuum of three developmental periods that correspond to intellectual growth and reasoning ability (Piaget, 1955). The first is the *sensorimotor period*, which starts at birth and ends at about 18 months. During this time, children are largely governed by reflexes, are extremely egocentric, and initially have little or no awareness of the world beyond their own physical sensations. Objects are deemed to have no existential reality for children during this period.

In addition, intellectual ability is viewed as being very limited. Children seem able to deal with only one task at a time, in a serial fashion, and they seem concerned only with functional success, with performance. Also, in Piaget's view they have no abstracting ability.

The second period, from 18 months to about 11 years, is the *concrete operational period*. Piaget (1955) divides it into two stages: the *preoperational stage*, which lasts until about age 7, and the *concrete operational stage*. This period is followed by the *formal operational period* beginning in early adolescence, which marks the development of adult reasoning ability.

In Piaget's analysis, during the preoperational stage children have very limited thinking ability and cannot reason abstractly. In addition, they find it difficult to take on the point of view or role of another. They cannot, in the words of Piaget (1955), "decenter," and as a result they are poor communicators. During the concrete operational stage, however, children's intellect becomes "operational," and they become much better at identifying and understanding changes in the world around them, which in turn helps them become better communicators.

Children focus their attention on their immediate surroundings and the people and objects they interact with daily. Piaget (1955) therefore characterizes the first stage of children's cognitive development as being concerned with constructing mental representations of reality and the cause-effect relationships that emerge from their daily interactions.

When children begin speaking at about age one, both cause-effect relationships and representations of reality are already well established. And as language does emerge, it reflects an object-related emphasis. That is, most of a child's first words are names of people and objects in the immediate environment (see Bates, 1976; Bates, Camaioni, & Volterra, 1975; MacNamara, 1972; Nelson, 1973). The order of development is quite clear in this respect: cognition related to people and things in the immediate environment leads to speech about those same people and things. From one culture to another, the pattern appears to be fairly consistent (see Bloom, L. 1970, 1973; Schlesinger, 1971), which suggests that intellectual development and language growth are uniform across cultures and backgrounds.

According to this model, language growth is linked to cognitive development. Children will be able to understand and produce increasingly complex utterances as they mature, because the mind becomes more adept at processing abstractions; the relationship is largely causal. The simple structure and content of basal readers reflect, in this analysis, the cognitive limitations that prohibit children from processing more complex texts.

There is a certain intuitive validity in these observations, and for decades the weight of Piaget's evidence strongly supported the view that cognition influences language. Nevertheless, work in developmental psychology over the last several years has significantly weakened this position, forcing a major reevaluation of Piaget's conclusions. Bates (1979), for example, investigating young children, found that cognitive knowledge did not always precede linguistic performance (also see Corrigan, 1978; Miller, Chapman, Branston, & Reichle, 1980). Rice and Kemper (1984), after reviewing numerous studies investigating the relationship between cognition and language conclude:

> Empirical support for a direct influence on formal linguistic structure in terms of children's emerging grammatical competencies remains to be demonstrated. . . . On a more specific level, the relevance of Piagetian sensorimotor tasks to language performance is questionable. (p. 29)

Currently, a majority of those working in the fields of cognitive development and psycholinguistics appear to agree that we cannot identify any *specific* influence cognition has on language. Instead, the influence may be very broad and nonspecific. If this conclusion is accurate, we must discard the common belief that we have to "teach children to think" before we can teach them to write.

Does Language Influence Cognition?

Lev Vygotsky (1962, 1978), like his contemporary Piaget, noted that at about age three young children begin to talk to themselves when doing things, as though giving verbal expression to their actions. Such talk is inherently different from the "conversations" they have been having for some time with others, because it seems to lack a social function. When playing with a doll, for example, children will make statements such as: "I'm going to wash the doll, then I'm going to get her dressed, and then I'm going to put her to sleep." Children generally make these utterances as though no one else can hear them, which led Vygotsky to refer to them as examples of "egocentric speech."

He proposed that egocentric speech marks the beginning of thought. Claims, assertions, examples, counterexamples, reasons—the building blocks of logical thought—are inherent in language, which is fundamentally a social action. In this account, the basic patterns of logical thought are evident in "social, collaborative forms of behavior" (1962: p. 19). Egocentric speech begins an internalization process by which socially determined behavior patterns are translated into what Vygotsky (1962) terms "inner speech," or thought. In his view, the origin of thought lies in social interactions expressed as speech, so the quality of a child's sociolinguistic environment will influence the quality of his or her thoughts.

As with Piaget, we immediately sense some truth in Vygotsky's analysis. Indeed, *Literacy and Bilingualism* has stressed repeatedly the importance of language as a social action as well as the extent to which discourse communities influence language. But it seems a huge and indefensible leap to suggest that the quality of language affects the quality of mind. Nevertheless, this view is widespread, especially in the humanities. In the next section, we look in detail at the issues associated with the humanistic perception.

The Humanist Position: Literacy Influences Mind

Several years ago, David Olson (1977) published a paper that has been quite influential among those who study writing. Taking Vygotsky's theoretical framework, Olson proposes an alternate version of the idea that language influences cognition. He argues that *literacy* produces a significant alteration in the modes of human thought. He claims that human history has reflected an evolution from speech to writing, from utterance to text, that has profoundly affected both the cultural and psychological development of mankind.

In Olson's analysis, writing in general, and the essay form in particular, account for the development of abstract thought; literacy is linked to heightened cognitive abilities. He argues, in fact, that people in nonliterate cultures are incapable of abstract thought. Writing develops abstracting ability because it forces people to decontextualize events (also see Ong, 1978). That is, it forces us to step outside the immediacy of a given situation and view it from alternative perspectives.

The result is a change in a person's perception of the world, which leads to cognitive growth and a change in the person. Olson (1977) states, for example, that "the emphasis on written prose . . . permitted the abstraction of logical procedures that could serve as the rules for thinking" (p. 267).

We see this line of thought reflected in the work of such diverse composition scholars as George Dillon (1981), E.D. Hirsch (1977), Walter Ong (1978, 1982), Leonard Scinto (1986), and Mina Shaughnessy (1977). Ong (1978), for example, states that "without writing . . . the mind simply cannot engage in [abstract] . . . thinking. . . . Without writing, the mind cannot even generate concepts such as 'history' or analysis . . ." (p. 39).

Too often this position has led to an "us-them" dichotomy that has been used to explain why certain bilingual students don't succeed in school. It suggests that children from backgrounds where written discourse may not be stressed will have cognitive deficiencies that will render them essentially incapable of academic achievement. The idea is that language-minority children suffer from "language deficits" that produce "cognitive deficiency."

Some Evidence for a Literacy Effect

The idea that literacy is linked to heightened cognitive skills received significant substantiation during the 1960s. During this period, a number of anthropologists attempted to explain why some cultures have reached a modern stage of development and why some haven't (see, for example, Finnegan, 1970; Goody, 1968, 1972; Goody & Watt, 1968; Greenfield, 1972; Levi-Strauss, 1966; Levy-Bruhl, 1975; Luria, 1976).

Researchers conducting these investigations would commonly give a group of nonliterate and usually non-Western subjects a task designed to measure cognitive abilities, then give the same task to a group of literate and usually Western subjects and compare the results. Colby and Cole (1976), for example, found that on tests of memory, nonliterate subjects from the Kpelle tribe in Africa performed far below the level of test subjects in the United States who were on average almost five years younger.

Luria (1976), a student of Vygotsky, found that the nonliterate subjects in his research had more difficulty categorizing and sorting objects than the literate subjects. They exhibited a method of cognitive processing that was essentially concrete and bound to the immediate situation.

This method of processing was evident, for example, when Luria presented pictures to subjects of a hammer, a saw, an ax, and a piece of lumber. When he asked which object did not belong with the others, the literate subjects quickly identified the piece of lumber, because it isn't a tool. The nonliterate subjects, on the other hand, could not understand the question. They insisted that all the objects went together; there was little use for a hammer, a saw, and an ax if there was no lumber to use in making something. Luria interpreted this response to mean that the nonliterates did not routinely establish abstract categories (e.g., tools) and that their abstracting ability was limited.

Evaluating the Evidence

To fully appreciate what is involved in research like Luria's, we have to distinguish between the significant effects language/literacy could have on cognition and the insignificant ones. The studies above suggest that literacy produces different ways of thinking and different behaviors. They have been used by writers like Olson (1977) and Ong (1978) to argue that literacy results in different states of being. Such states would qualify as significant effects because they are linked to *conceptual capacity* (see Lakoff, 1987, for a full discussion). In Ong's analysis, for example, the nonliterate person is *incapable* of abstract thought. In the context of negative bilingualism, the view is that linguistic confusion leads to cognitive confusion, which in turn is detrimental to intellectual capacity.

On the other hand, we know there are specific cultural characteristics related to accepting the attributes objects may have in common (see Rosch, 1978). The often-cited differences between English and Eskimo regarding the number of words used to describe "snow" illustrate this point: Eskimo uses different words to distinguish between wet snow and dry snow (as well as many other types) because such distinctions are important in a land covered by snow most of the year. Eskimo therefore includes category attributes that are generally ignored in English, although they do exist in English. Skiers, for example, have numerous terms to describe snow in its various states, and there is much overlap between the English terms and the Eskimo. We can conclude, then, that even within a single culture there will be clusters of shared attributes that vary by gender, occupation, hobbies, socioeconomic status, and so forth.

Lakoff (1987) explains this variation succinctly when he tells us that "Human beings do not function with internally consistent, monolithic conceptual systems" (p. 305). Nevertheless, in the context of positive bilingualism, we find a view of just such a monolithic system that bilingualism supposedly eliminates. That is, it is commonly assumed that the monolingual has a single (and implicitly limited) conceptual system that bilingualism remedies by supplying a second (see, for example, Cummins & Swain, 1986; Genesee, 1987).

It should be clear, however, that alternative conceptual systems cannot count as a significant language/cognition effect. There are, for instance, no major cognitive consequences associated with having a large number of words for snow. The reason is straightforward: if a person has only one word, he or she has the *capacity* for acquiring and using more should the need or desire arise, as in the case of skiers and snow. In this account, Luria's findings reported above could simply be an instance of the nonliterate group's refusal to accept the category attributes that Luria implicitly designated, not a demonstration of an inability to establish abstract categories. The issue becomes one of a conceptual system, not conceptual capacity. That is, the subjects he interviewed could have adopted his conceptual system, his way of looking at the world, if they had been motivated or perhaps even asked explicitly to do so. In that case, they would have stated that the piece of lumber was not a tool.

The problem with most of the studies that attempt to characterize the relationship between mental processes and language/literacy is that they confuse conceptual capacity and conceptual systems. As a result, researchers like those mentioned above have made a fundamental mistake. They have explained the absence in nonliterate cultures of certain abstract categories commonly found among literate, especially Western, cultures as indicating a lack of abstracting ability rather than as the presence of an alternative conceptual system, even when evidence of abstracting ability abounds. For example, every recorded culture, whether literate or nonliterate, has (or had) some form of religious beliefs (see Campbell, 1959). Religion by its very nature is highly abstract. We also know that collective terms similar to "tools" in Luria's study are used in every recorded language to designate groups of people and things (Ullmann, 1963). But different conceptual systems will result in different things being designated as "tools."

We find a related problem in the fact that researchers who compile the anthropological data during the 1960s consistently conflated literacy and schooling (see Scribner & Cole, 1981). The significance of this flaw in methodology becomes clear when we consider that classroom activities inherently involve decontextualization, and they emphasize nonfunctional intellectual experiences. In other words, they essentially train students to engage in alternative ways of conceptualizing reality. As a result, there is no way to determine whether the findings from these studies reflect the effects of literacy or the effects of schooling. The observed differences, in other words, may be associated with education, not literacy.

In the case of Luria (1976), the groups he compared were not merely literates and nonliterates but were literates with schooling and nonliterates without. These factors lead Scribner and Cole (1981) to state that such studies "fail to support the specific claims made for literacy's effects. . . . No comparisons were ever made between children with and children without a written language" (pp. 11–12).

Scribner and Cole's investigation is the most detailed ever made of literacy's effects on cognition. Their research was conducted among the Vai, a group of people in West Africa who developed an independent writing system early in the nineteenth century. The Vai script is used regularly for notes and letters, but there is no body of literature written in the script. Only about half of the people who are literate in the Vai script have had some formal schooling, which means that there was a large group of literate but unschooled subjects to draw on.

Over a four-year period, the researchers evaluated over 1,000 subjects, and their findings seriously challenge the view that language influences cognition. After examining a wide range of cognitive and linguistic behaviors, Scribner and Cole found only four variables that showed any influence. Literates outperformed the nonliterates in: (1) synthesizing a spoken message, (2) using graphic symbols to represent language, (3) using language as a means of instruction, and (4) talking about correct Vai speech. These areas of performance are not significant in terms of behavior, and in fact the nature of literacy would cause us to expect such differences.

More important, the researchers found *no cognitive superiority* when comparing literates with nonliterates. There were no data to suggest that literacy is linked to abstracting ability or cognitive growth. Summarizing this aspect of their investigation, Scribner and Cole report:

> Our results are in direct conflict with persistent claims that "deep psychological differences" divide literate and nonliterate populations. . . . On no task—logic, abstraction, memory, communication—did we find all nonliterates performing at lower levels than all literates. (p. 251)

The weight of Scribner and Cole's research, along with criticism similar to what we've presented in this section, has been overwhelming for a large number of teachers and writers. Even David Olson has changed his mind, and you will recall that he was a strongly influential advocate of the language-influences-cognition view (see Olson, 1987). Unfortunately, much damage has already been done, and few people are aware that early advocates like Olson have shifted their positions. This lack of awareness seems especially acute in bilingual education.

One Theory but Two Outcomes?

In concluding our analysis of the idea that language influences cognition, we would suggest that teachers should find it troubling that attitudes toward bilingualism are fairly evenly divided. As we've already noted, some scholars and teachers see bilingualism as positive. Cummins and Swain (1986), for example, argue that bilingualism increases a person's awareness of language and gives one the ability to process experiences from two different points of view, which they argue provides bilinguals with an inherent advantage over monolinguals (also see Hakuta, 1986). In their analysis, more points of view equals more knowledge or awareness, so bilingualism is beneficial. Other scholars and teachers, however, see it as negative. Sanchez (1987), for example, notes the tendency of bilinguals to mix English and Spanish, and he argues that such mixing signifies linguistic confusion that in turn causes cognitive confusion (also see Hakuta, 1986). In this view, the low academic achievement of, say, Hispanics is tied to bilingualism's harmful (i.e., confusing) cognitive consequences.

These two contrary views also affect perceptions of linguistic transfer. In assessing the influence L_1 exerts on L_2, those who see positive consequences in bilingualism are inclined to argue that the lexical, logical, and rhetorical features of the first language transfer positively to the second. That is, the first language functions to inform and support second-language learning. Those who see negative consequences, however, argue that L_1 hinders L_2. This latter perception is most commonly expressed through the idea of first-language interference, and it is quite widespread, particularly in composition studies. The idea is that the difficulties bilingual students have with writing can be attributed to language patterns in L_1 that prevent them from achieving competency in L_2.

Curiously enough, these two fundamentally opposed positions are both driven by the same theory—that language influences cognition. Language is seen as having either positive or negative consequences for how the mind functions. Having two incompatible views emerge from the same theory is unacceptable because the purpose of a theory is to help arrive at a consistent description of a phenomenon. If it generates contradictory descriptions, a theory is inadequate because of inherent flaws or because it is being applied with insufficient rigor.

Finding a Reciprocal Relationship

In many respects, the two views of language and cognition we've been discussing are like the old problem of the chicken and the egg—we can't really determine which comes first. It may well be, however, that the claims of causality inherent in these views are inappropriate. That is, no causality exists. Instead, language and cognition are largely autonomous systems that develop simultaneously (see Glass, Holyoak, & Santa, 1979; Johnson-Laird, 1983; Rice & Kemper, 1984). Each has some marginal influence on the other, in a reciprocal relationship, because in the final analysis language is part of the totality we call mind.

In our view, debating the extent even of this marginal influence misses the point, which is that teachers ought to be concerned with the totality because their goal is to improve both how children think and how they use language.

PLANS AND GOALS: APPLYING THE MIND/LANGUAGE FRAMEWORK

When given the opportunity to address complex topics and issues, too many students deal with them simplistically, never venturing beyond the trite or passé. In these cases, we may indeed want to equate poor writing with poor thinking. It is important to understand, however, that the relationship is not causal. We can attribute the poor writing as well as the poor thinking primarily to experiential, motivational, educational, and even rhetorical factors. Poor writing is unlikely to have a single cause but is probably the result of a complex array of variables. Not knowing how to perceive the world in a way that goes beyond obvious sensory impressions—which is an experiential as well as an educational issue—may be one of them. Having the desire to perceive the world in a way that goes beyond just surface appearances and then having the desire to communicate that perception to others in writing are certainly two others. After all, considering life's complexities is hard work, and its rewards are generally intangible. Students need some form of motivation if they are to develop the desire to think.

Unraveling motivation, however, is extremely difficult, in part because for years it has been interpreted in language arts to mean that teachers are obliged to keep students entertained and to provide reading and writing tasks that are "fun." The mistake is fundamental. Stressing that learning must be fun confuses the issues and ignores completely what is at stake. It offers no incentive or mechanism to help students become self-motivated; in fact, it offers a harmful model that suggests hard work, discipline, and perseverance are antithetical to the educational experience. In other words, by stressing immediate gratification, it encourages students to seek out the superficial and to adopt simplistic perspectives regarding the world around them.

We know that the key to successful learning lies in developing students' intrinsic motivation to accomplish a task. Sandra Mano's (1986) research indicates that successful writers are those who, for unknown reasons, *want to define themselves as writers*. They have an experience with a poem, an essay, a novel, or a film that causes them to decide that they would like to produce something similar and share it with others. To help themselves accomplish this goal, they become intense consumers of whatever genre they want to produce: they will read novel after novel or poem after poem, or they will view a particular kind of film again and again. Reading, for example, becomes a means of discovering more about the discourse form they wish to imitate, such that reading and writing are reciprocal activities. In the context of bilingual education, we must rephrase Mano's conclusion such that successful bilingual writers are those who want to define themselves as writers *in two languages*.

Mano's research should cause us to look critically at teachers' efforts to make reading and writing more meaningful through specifying the rhetorical context of an assignment. The aim in most cases is to provide an audience or a purpose for the task. As well intentioned as this approach may be, we must recognize that real reading and writing tasks arise out of very specific needs, commonly in the workplace, that allow people to know both the audience and the purpose.

When it comes to writing, many teachers perceive that language-minority students may have greater difficulty constructing an audience and a purpose for a paper written in English, so they specify these in the assignment. But any purpose the teacher specifies will always be her purpose, not the students'. This fact suggests that in the context of the language arts classroom, the writing tasks we provide for students cannot avoid being somewhat arhetorical. Our teaching is therefore going to be subject to a perpetual tension between what we hope to achieve on the one hand (rhetorical activities) and the constraints created by the basically artificial language environment of the classroom.

On the cognitive level, we can describe some of what writing entails and thereby get a clearer understanding of what we must do in view of those constraints. For example, Steve Witte (1985) suggests that when writers decide to compose, whether on their own or because of a teacher's assignment, they formulate an internal "pre-text" that has both global and local discourse features. The former consist of such things as audience, intention, and genre conventions. The latter consist of such things as sentence structure, spelling, and lexicon. Planning an essay would therefore involve a complex process of formulation, monitoring, and revision of the pre-text. The actual writing (pen to paper) would largely be the translation of an already revised pre-text. It seems certain, however, that the more thought that goes into modeling the pre-text the better the actual composition will be. In this account, we may understand why experienced writers usually revise drafts of a composition less than their inexperienced counterparts and still produce better writing. They have performed more revision during planning.

Flower and Hayes (1981) and Matsuhashi (1981) have determined that good writers spend comparatively less time considering surface features when planning a pre-text than do poor writers. The implication for teaching is that teachers should help students focus more attention on planning at the global level and less at the sentence level. They will want to develop activities that not only provide practice reflecting on events and ideas but also lead to the development of pre-texts with global, rhetorical characteristics.

We would suggest that there is another stage of the discourse plan that comes before the pre-text and that it consists of nonverbal mental models of experience, what we referred to earlier as "mental representations of reality." Language is in part a process by which words and syntax are mapped onto these models. We can predict that this process is inherently more demanding for bilinguals than for monolinguals because of the two channels, L_1 and L_2, available for mapping. When they reach the pre-text stage, there are likely to be significant gaps at the local level as a result of insufficient vocabulary and incomplete mastery of English grammar. There are also likely to be gaps at the global level, largely because students are focusing their attention, often with the teacher's encouragement, on surface features.

PRELITERATE STUDENTS

We define preliterate students as those who have not yet learned to read and write in any language. This category includes a number of possibilities. First, there are students age five and under whose parents have not provided meaningful encounters with print and who, as a result, have not learned to read or write before entering school. This group includes the majority of children starting school at the kindergarten and first-grade levels.

Second, there are students who may be older than five or six, who have never attended school and have not been taught to read and write at home. This may be the case of immigrant children from war zones or secluded rural areas where it was impossible to go to school, if a school were available at all. In addition, some children of migrant laborers are in this category.

Third, there are students who are on their way to becoming literate, but are not quite there yet. For example, second- and third-grade students would also fit in this category, even though they may have acquired a number of decoding and encoding skills in their native language, may have enough comprehension skills for their grade-level texts, and may be able to write brief compositions. However, their overall level of literacy is quite low.

In the preliterate category we include those students with physical and mental handicaps that may have prevented them from learning to read and write in their native language. These are students who qualify for special education placement. Although this is a group that we will not address in this text, it is important for the teacher to be able to distinguish between student placement in special education programs owing to legitimate handicaps and placement owing to misconceptions of the nature of language proficiency.

In the past, inability to speak English was viewed as a deficiency. Therefore, many students who were not proficient in English were erroneously assigned to special education programs. Even now it is not uncommon to find students in special education who are behind academically as a result of unsystematic bilingual education programs, inappropriate instruction, or early reclassification. The necessity for careful assessment is clear. (See Cummins, 1983, for a thorough discussion of special education students and bilingual education.)

Although a detailed discussion is beyond the scope of this text, we also include in the preliterate category adults who have never attended school or who attended school but are functionally illiterate. This group may consist of mostly older immigrants who do not speak English and who were illiterate in their native language upon arrival in the United States; it may also include the children of these immigrants, now older, who somehow never learned to read and write.

Teaching Approaches for Preliterate Students

With preliterates, as with literates and postliterates, certain teaching approaches will be more appropriate than others. In the next chapter, we discuss in greater detail these approaches as they apply to each literacy area. At this point, however, we focus our discussion on applying the bilingual education program goals and assumptions and on making a distinction among preliterates for instructional purposes.

Students who do not speak English will be assigned to one of the language programs available at the local school, most likely a bilingual education program. The program goals and implementation will vary according to whether the local philosophy is pro-enrichment and native-language maintenance or pro-transition to English and compensatory. Thus, with preliterate students, the teacher has the option to use the students' native language to the extent possible or perhaps not to use it at all.

Generally, within bilingual program goals and guidelines, preliterate students begin to read and write in their native language. At the same time, they learn English as a second language and all subject matter such as math and social science in their native language. The program continues systematically until the students are reclassified as proficient in English. Figure 5.1 illustrates this process.

The model provided in Figure 5.1 describes ideal circumstances, where a full range of teaching resources is available. The teachers are bilingual and are credentialed for bilingual instruction. The school has materials for instruction in the native language as well as English.

Unfortunately, this ideal is not always achieved. Some schools lack the resources for instruction in the students' native language. In this situation,

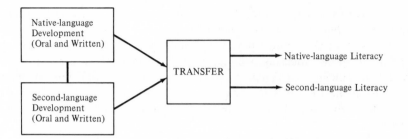

Figure 5.1. Instructional Process for Preliterate Students

English is used initially and the native language is used only as a support via the paraprofessional aide to teach reading and writing and oral language development.

When dealing with preliterate non-English-speaking students, teachers may need to modify the traditional curriculum to provide adequate instruction. The following questions can serve as guides to help with such modification:

1. Will I begin to teach this child to read and write in his native language?
2. What methods will I use?
3. How will I teach this child to speak English?
4. How will I teach him the content-area curriculum?
5. To what extent will I use the native language and English throughout the school day?

These questions are answered differently depending on resources available and on district policy. For example, if the teacher is bilingual and literate in the children's language, the answer to the first question may unequivocally be "yes." If the teacher does not speak the language and if the policy of the school district requires initial native-language instruction, the question becomes "who will?" Usually the answer would have to be "another teacher in a team or the paraprofessional."

The question of appropriate methods depends on the age and maturity of the children. With young preliterates, teachers will want to focus instruction on oral language development in both the native language and English at different times of the day, so that both languages will be kept separate. Activities for students may include listening to stories, giving story dictations to the teacher that they will then read back, reading in the native language through both "language experience" and decoding, group story writing and reading back in either the native language or English.

For content-area instruction, teachers cannot rely on existing instructional materials designed for mainstream language speakers. They will have to place more emphasis on students' understanding the message. Manipulative and visual materials will be very valuable in content-area instruction. Science can be taught via experiments, social studies via constructing models, language via creative dramatics, or music and math via manipulators. "Turn to page such and such in your textbooks" will no longer have any meaning. In actuality, a more exciting way of teaching and learning will result from this approach than from the more passive textbook/workbook method.

With older preliterates, materials will vary to accommodate the needs of a more mature audience. The approach may be the same; however, the pace of the lesson may be faster, because older learners will have longer attention spans. Both the content and the context of the lesson will have to appeal and be relevant to this learner.

LITERATE STUDENTS

The literate category comprises the largest number of students. We will consider students literate if they can read and write in their native language at the fourth-grade level. Although this reading level is essentially arbitrary, it seems appropriate because it represents a threshold level that allows students to access texts written for high school students.

These texts are generally written at the sixth-grade level, so a grade level of four indicates that students will be able to process high school texts, although they may have some difficulty. This threshold level of literacy also allows students to process most of the texts they encounter on a daily basis outside school, but it denies them easy access to certain sources of information, such as major newspapers, which tend to be written at about the tenth-grade level. It is important to stress, however, that the threshold level, or even the average high school level (about grade 8.5–9.0 for graduating seniors) will not allow students access to more sophisticated texts and as such may not be considered academic literacy.

At this level, students are likely to possess and apply reading and writing mechanics, using the syntax and grammar of their native language, and they are also likely to know subject matter content, such as history, geography, mathematics, and social studies. Students' knowledge will vary according to the quality and extent of instruction received and to their ability to retain and apply what was taught.

Many immigrants fit this category, such as those students who attended school in their native country or who were taught at home and now live in a new country with parents in search of political asylum, business opportunities, or business growth. Students in this category have the potential to do very well in school using a second language, but they could also be at risk if appropriate instruction is not provided.

Teaching Approaches for Literate Students

Instruction for literate students should take into account the following: (1) transfer of knowledge from the native language to English in content-area instruction, (2) new content-area knowledge, (3) instruction in English language, (4) continuation of native-language development in reading and writing, and (5) transfer of knowledge in native-language reading and writing as far as it is linguistically transferable to English. Figure 5.2 illustrates how these factors are interrelated.

For this group of students, assessment in the native-language reading and writing skills and in content-matter knowledge is particularly important, as it is the only way teachers may know what can transfer to English, what new content needs to be taught, and how much instruction in the native language will be necessary.

If students are literate in their native language and are at or close to grade level in content matter, teachers can proceed with the grade-level curriculum, emphasize instruction in English as a second language, and teach new content areas either in English or in the native language. If English is used as the medium of instruction for content, the teacher must ensure that the concepts are clearly

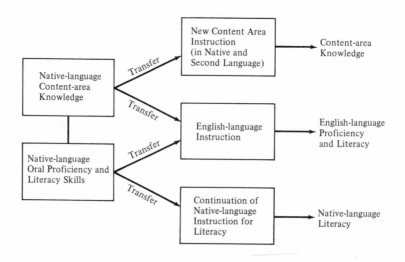

Figure 5.2. Instructional Process for Literate Students

understood. High context clues and manipulators will be important when teaching new content material in English.

For these students, instruction in English as a second language should go beyond oral communication and should incorporate reading and writing. A translation method that uses literary works in English or in the students' native language is particularly appropriate to make students literate in English. Linguistic connections between the native language and English are also useful for literacy in English.

The students' knowledge of content-area material can be very useful in teaching reading and writing in English. For example, let us suppose that students know about volcanos in their native language. Teachers can extract a chapter on volcanos from an English text in science and can have the students learn the English vocabulary that pertains to volcanoes. The students can translate the content from English to their native language and can use it to learn the structure and form of English sentences, all within a context they understand. They can do experiments on volcano eruptions by building a volcano together with English-speaking students in a cooperative learning group. They can write their observations of the experiment in English, formulate hypotheses, and draw conclusions, all in English.

POSTLITERATE STUDENTS

Our final category comprises students we are calling postliterate. These students are older, perhaps high school or college age, and have attended school in their native countries. They have a broad knowledge of subject-matter content as well as reading and writing skills in their native language. They are more mature students, with the highest potential to achieve academic success in English.

Teaching Approaches for Postliterate Students

The instructional process for these students would include a process similar to the one described for literate students, with adaptations for content and student maturity. Figure 5.3 illustrates the related instructional factors.

Given the higher level of knowledge these students bring to the classroom, teachers can place less emphasis on new content and more on English instruction, focusing on reading, writing, and oral communication. Teachers can use literary works students know as the basis for English instruction. We recommend a method in which students translate from English to their native language. Lessons should focus on cuing devices that help comprehension, using context to construct meaning, and on analysis of sentence patterns. Teachers can formulate questions for students to answer in English, based on this content. They can also derive dialogues that students can use with one another to practice oral communication.

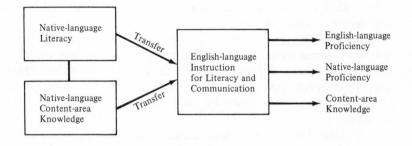

Figure 5.3. Instructional Process for Postliterate Students

MOTIVATION, STUDENT INTEREST, AND AGE

Students in the three categories above require different teaching methods. Obviously, there will be differences in teaching approaches even within the categories. What will be appropriate for five-year-old, language-minority students who are nonliterate in their native language will be quite inappropriate for the nonliterate teenager or young adult.

Students' ages and their native-language literacy levels are important factors in determining appropriate teaching methods. Students may be assigned to a particular grade because of their age, but that does not mean they have commensurate literacy skills. They may have skills above or below their assigned grade. Their subject-area knowledge likewise may be above or below grade level.

For example, one of the authors of this text found that many of her fifth-grade students, newly arrived from Soviet Armenia, had a knowledge of geography that far exceeded the knowledge of geography possessed by mainstream English-speaking students. When the school's Armenian advisors investigated, they found that geography is a subject strongly emphasized in elementary schools in Soviet Armenia, which accounted for the students' superior knowledge. With this information, she was able to help teachers modify the curriculum to avoid teaching the Armenian students material they already knew.

But age is important in other respects, especially in regard to second-language acquisition. It is widely believed, for example, that younger children learn a second language much more quickly than older children and adults. John Schumann (1978) and others, however, have shown that age does not seem to be a particularly important factor in mastering a second language. Schumann suggests that acculturation—the availability of social and psychological contacts with mainstream speakers—affects adult second-language learning more than age. (Other social and affective factors have also been identified that discredit the notion that age per se plays a significant role in language learning. (See Harley, 1986, for an in-depth discussion.)

Although the research suggests that there is no age that is particularly propitious for learning a second language, age does appear to affect academic achievement, in so far as the students have a stronger background in their native language. The more mature students who have achieved a certain level of literacy in their native language transfer this knowledge to the second language at a much faster rate than do students who lack a strong background. These students perform at a higher level academically (Cummins, 1988).

Age, although not significant in the neurological maturation sense, is significant in a pedagogical sense, in terms of what teachers can do to elicit students' interests and to keep them on task. Thus it is a factor that teachers must consider when planning lessons.

A 6-year-old preliterate student, for example, will need an instructional approach significantly different from the approach used with a 10-year-old preliterate. The 6-year-old will have a shorter attention span and be interested in different types of things. The 6-year-old will require lessons that involve shorter, hands-on activities that allow movement and interaction with the material. The older students will be able to remain on task for a longer period of time, so the lesson may be longer.

Interest in the task at hand will also differ between the older and younger preliterates. Motivation theory suggests that successful lessons are developed from the interests of the children and are related to their background. Madeline Hunter (1970a, 1970b, 1982), for example, tells us that before teachers introduce a new concept to students, they must elicit the students' interest first. This can be done by asking questions about the students' experience on the topic, by showing motivational materials such as an interesting artifact, a book, a film, or simply by making connections to previous learning. There is no reason to think that these principles, which apply without question to mainstream students, should not apply also to nonmainstream students.

Motivation and student interest should, if anything, be emphasized in the instructional program for nonmainstream language speakers. Although mainstream speakers will readily relate to the topic, because they understand the language of instruction, nonmainstream speakers will have to depend on context clues to understand the essence of the lessons. This will require more attention and ability on their part to remain on task. Therefore, if they are not interested or motivated to participate, the lesson will be nothing but meaningless noise. Students who have lost interest may begin daydreaming, or they may become behavior problems and cause disruptions in the classroom.

Topics, materials, and motivational techniques used by the teacher to elicit interest from the child will have to suit the developmental age and interests of the child. While the 6-year-old will find *The Cat in the Hat* particularly fascinating, the 10-year-old will prefer a Nintendo game for entertainment. The content of *Winnie the Pooh* will be beneath the dignity of a 12-year-old preliterate, but just right for the younger student. And the content of certain basal preprimers will be offensive to the more sophisticated, albeit preliterate child, but may be appropriate to the very young child.

Unfortunately, materials that have high interest for older students and low readability level are not abundant. Often teachers must carefully select or even prepare their own materials so older preliterates will be interested in the topic of the lesson, motivated to participate, and get the appropriate practice to learn from it.

Social studies textbooks, for example, are written at the readability level of mainstream students at the particular grade level for which the text is intended. These texts are clearly not appropriate for older, nonmainstream, preliterate students. If the interest level is correct, the readability level will not be.

This situation will require that teachers either use audiovisuals to convey the message from the text and forgo the text altogether, use materials in the students' native language, if available, or develop new materials. The teachers will have to shoulder much responsibility in this case. However, having the students stare at a text they cannot read will not teach the students anything except tolerance and endurance under adverse conditions, hardly reasons for their coming to school!

In most cases it is easier for teachers to deal with younger preliterates than with older ones. The materials available, even when not in the children's native language, will not contain much written text and will be more congruent with the children's developmental age and interest level than materials for older students.

In social studies, for example, when teachers want to use the text, after the lesson has been covered through hands-on activities, all they will have to do is convey the text's message and teach the written material as part of reading instruction within the content area. Once the message is understood, through previous activities within the same topic, students will be ready for the printed word and able to assimilate it. Thus students will have learned not only the content material but also reading within a meaningful context.

When the gap between available materials and student age is wider, it is more difficult for the teacher. However, the maturity level of the student is an advantage here. Teachers may use the same approach we suggested above for younger preliterates, and when the time comes for the printed word of the text to be taught, the students will have the longer attention span and maturity to understand and remember lengthier written material.

SOCIOECONOMIC AND CULTURAL BACKGROUND

Whenever we talk about bilingualism and instructional programs in various languages, we are also dealing with at least two cultures, the mainstream culture and the culture of the immigrant. Because many immigrants are in fact members of the lower socioeconomic class and arrive in the new country in search of a better life, invariably there are conflicts. To some people, it will seem to follow that the immigrants' culture is not good enough.

The immigrants are existing between the old and the new values and must make choices: to adapt, reject, accept, and select norms and mores to live by in the new country. The mainstream culture holds opinions of the immigrants, and they may not always be favorable. The temptation on the part of the mainstream culture to categorize and classify the immigrants according to values they are perceived to hold can become detrimental to the newcomers' success. The interactions between the two cultures may cause misunderstandings and even friction when their expectations of one another are not congruent. The school, being part of the mainstream society, will be the field where many of the feelings, expectations, and frictions may be played.

Research indicates that students from the higher socioeconomic classes often do better in school; that some cultural values held by certain cultures help the new arrivals acculturate and succeed in the new country better than the values held by other cultures; and that members of certain cultures succeed while others do not. Some research actually identifies which cultures do better than others, arguing that it is because of their intrinsic superiority (Dunn, 1987). The context within which the new immigrants attempt to operate is not necessarily examined or called into question.

The problem with this line of research is that it leads to the stereotyping of nonmainstream cultures. It also leads to blaming the nonmainstream students for their lack of achievement because of the cultural values they hold. We know that if a parent or another adult helps the children with homework nightly, the children will probably do better in school. However, to associate this practice with the success of a certain culture and to generalize that low socioeconomic classes or single-parent families do not help their children with homework (therefore the children do poorly in school) is superficial and dysfunctional at the very least.

We have friends, as an example, who are both medical doctors, mainstream parents. Because they are so busy with their careers, they did not follow their kindergarten child's progress in school as they might have, had they not been so busy. They suddenly realized with horror, upon being summoned to school by the teacher, that their child was the only one in class who could not read. All the time the child had brought home the ''poem of the week'' from school, she received the response: ''How nice, a poem of the week!'' from the parents. They never realized that the teacher's intention in giving that poem was that the parents help the child memorize it, as the poem was crucial to the reading activities for the week. Thus the child was being penalized in school for not having done her homework. Once the expectation was made clear, the problem was immediately resolved, and the child is now a happy reader.

We give this example to illustrate that it may not be only low socioeconomic classes that do not help children with their homework. Teacher expectations play an important part. Because the teacher did not expect this lack of interest from these parents, the problem was resolved. If the teacher had held lower expectations of this child's ability and of her parents, and had she not followed through with a home call, the child might have suffered an academic setback.

Sometimes society's stereotyping of minority cultures leads to cultural frictions and misunderstanding of expectations. It is important, therefore, that teachers be knowledgeable enough to maintain an open mind and in turn focus on helping all students succeed in school. As we stated earlier, rather than looking for reasons to explain why students cannot achieve, spend the same amount of energy thinking of ways you can, as the teacher, provide the environment that builds upon the culture of the children in a positive way to help them succeed.

CONCLUSION

This chapter analyzed a range of work that has attempted to describe a relationship between bilingualism and intelligence. The majority of the research on this topic has assumed a causal relationship, which currently seems unwarranted. A clearer understanding of how mind and language interact suggests that claims of causality are both inappropriate and misdirected. That is, bilingualism as a phenomenon has neither positive nor negative effects on intelligence.

At the heart of this conclusion are current perceptions concerning the relationship between mind and language. The view that bilingualism has either positive or negative consequences for intelligence is tied to the widely held notion that language influences cognition. Research over the last dozen years clearly demonstrates, however, that this notion is misconceived. At best, we can describe a reciprocal relationship between language and cognition, in that they exert some mutual, minimal influence on each other.

This chapter also identified, in terms of native language literacy, the student population teachers are likely to encounter. We suggested three categories, the *preliterate*, the *literate*, and the *postliterate* students and began giving a general overview of instructional options the teacher may exercise.

We identified and discussed issues of a socio-psychological nature, which will be of significant consideration for teachers. One is the issue of age, a factor in academic achievement in the second language, which influences pedagogical approaches; the other is the issue of culture, a factor of extreme importance in intergroup relations and in teacher expectations.

We found two issues that contribute to age being of particular significance to teachers. One is the native-language literacy issue. More important than in the neurological sense, age is important in so far as the students have commensurate literacy background in their native language. The older the students are on arrival, the stronger their literacy level in their native language, provided that they have had the opportunity to attend school. Thus, age is important only in so far as it is related to literacy level in the native language. As a result, we emphasized the necessity of native-language assessment before the instructional program is established.

The other side of the age issue is age as a factor in pedagogical approaches in relation to student interests and motivation. To make instruction as relevant and interesting to the students as possible, the teachers will have to account for developmental age as it impacts student interest and motivation in order to maximize learning.

Finally, we discussed how cultural issues enter into the instructional process in ways that may be detrimental to the academic achievement of the students. We recommended that teachers attempt to remain open-minded in the face of stereotyping the nonmainstream culture and focus on pedagogical factors they can control.

In this context, it is extremely important for teachers to recognize that no relationship exists between intelligence and bilingualism. Although it may be human nature to equate language skills with mental ability, there is no direct correlation, and in fact, the errors bilingual students make during reading and writing tasks are indicative of developmental gaps that necessarily occur when people master a second language.

CHAPTER 6

Teaching Language in Context

OVERVIEW

This chapter focuses on a range of topics related to teaching English in a meaningful context. It begins with an analysis of the various methods currently available for teaching a second language. It analyzes the more prominent approaches, noting their strengths and weaknesses. Overall, these methods are inadequate in meeting the goal of academic achievement because they concentrate exclusively on developing either literacy skills or oral proficiency. None offers an approach that integrates the skills bilingual students need to succeed.

In view of this deficiency, the chapter outlines an approach that provides a "whole-language," literature-based methodology for teaching literacy and language. The remainder of the chapter is devoted to examining some of the ways this approach can be used with preliterate, literate, and postliterate students.

TEACHING METHODS FOR SECOND-LANGUAGE INSTRUCTION

Various methods for teaching second languages have been developed over the years. Most of those we outline here have been influenced by numerous schools of thought, such as structural linguistics, behavioral psychology, cognitive psychology, and humanistic education, each of which also influenced general educational methodology. As a result, the approaches to teaching language summarized below are based on quite different assumptions and goals.

The Grammar-Translation Method

The grammar-translation method has been used for centuries. Students begin translating simple texts in the second language, and they gradually move on to more advanced texts. They are expected to translate and comprehend what they read by applying studied grammar rules and vocabulary lists and by using a dictionary.

Two assumptions often associated with this method are that mental discipline is essential to strengthen the mind and that translating texts is a means of instilling such discipline. The grammar-translation method was traditionally used to teach the classical languages, Latin and Greek. An important goal was for students to become acquainted with great literary works, so the approach was often deemed more scholarly than other language teaching methods. There is some merit in this goal: interpreting meaning and analyzing literary works in terms of their artistic and historic value have intrinsic worth.

Nevertheless, the translation approach has been criticized on the grounds that it does not allow students the opportunity to use the target language in oral communication. And indeed, as we can personally attest, having been the recipients of such instruction in our own foreign-language learning, this method consists of often tedious analyses and the memorization of grammatical rules that are rarely applied in a modern, conversational context. There is usually no concern even for how the written language is pronounced. Typically, the result is that the students can read and interpret literary works written in the language, but they cannot speak it.

This method is used not only for learning defunct languages but is widely used outside the United States to teach modern foreign languages, particularly English. Students don't learn to converse with one another; rather they translate Shakespeare, *Beowulf*, the *Canterbury Tales*, *Huckleberry Finn*, and so forth and they work extensively on grammar exercises.

The Audio-lingual Method

Now very much out of favor, the audio-lingual method was used for many years in the United States with minority-language students for ESL instruction and with native-English speakers in foreign-language classes. The main goal was always oral communication. Based on the behavioralist assumption that language is essentially a matter of habit, this method utilizes repetition of regular language patterns, commonly in conjunction with a "language lab," to produce automatic responses in the target language. Drills, memorization, and substitution of patterns are the major techniques to establish habit (see Brooks, 1964; Lardo, 1957).

For example, students might begin with the language pattern "I have a book." They would then be taught to substitute the vocabulary word "book" with other object words, such as "pen," "pencil," and "paper," and learn the pattern and vocabulary by repeating the sentences over and over. The articles *a* and *an* would be included in the various substitutions. Students would be asked, "What do you have?" and they would have to respond appropriately with "I have a (or an) _____." Another example of a substitution drill is the response to the question, "What does she (or he) have?" Students would have to distinguish aurally the difference between *he* and *she* and *has* and *have* and then respond appropriately with "She (or He) has _____."

Having used this method with students, we can attest that it can be stultifying and boring. As indicated above, it tends to focus on local features (pronouns and verb forms) rather than on global features (purpose, intention, and audience) of language, and students seem to lose interest quickly. After months of practicing, they may still know very little of the essence and vocabulary of the language. After endless repetition, students may still not be able to transfer what they have learned during pattern practice to a conversation. As a result, in a natural language setting students may use both the incorrect pronoun (*he* or *she*) and the incorrect verb form (*have* or *has*).

In addition, because this method is predicated on habit formation, students seem to divorce themselves from their own verbal utterances and are limited to responding parrotlike to verbal stimuli provided by a teacher or a tape. Meaning and creativity in self-expression are rare because they aren't stressed. Moreover, students have little opportunity to develop literacy skills in the target language.

The Direct Method

An opposite approach to grammar translation is the direct method, currently used primarily with foreign-language instruction for older students in secondary schools or college. No translation is allowed in this method. Instead, students are expected to understand the meaning of what is said directly from the language they are learning, without translating it into their native language. The goal is to communicate orally, so great emphasis is placed on developing vocabulary, on correct pronunciation, and on conversation.

Grammatical rules are learned inductively; that is, students make generalizations on the basis of the language model the teacher provides. We don't find explanations of grammar. For example, a teacher might read a passage in the target language and then ask students if they have any questions about its meaning. If students say they don't know what certain phrases mean, the teacher uses objects or audiovisuals to get the meaning across without explaining or translating into the native language. It is up to students to ask questions that will elicit discovery of general grammatical rules that they can conceptualize, formulate, and then apply in later language production.

This approach requires students to engage in active, analytical mental processes as the discussion in the target language proceeds. Necessarily, students must be both motivated and linguistically sophisticated. If they don't know what to ask, or if, as happens normally, they work on processing for meaning rather than structure, they may not arrive at generalizations of grammatical rules and may not be able to generate new language by applying those rules that allow us to produce discourse. Matters are further complicated by the fact that in languages like English, meaning is frequently linked to syntax, as in "Fred was drowning" and "Fred drowned." Understanding the difference between these sentences hinges on understanding something about participles.

A clear difficulty inherent in this method, therefore, is the absence of any explicit discussion of the rules and conventions that govern the target language. As a result, students are likely to speak incorrectly or generally misuse the language owing to misinterpretation or misapplication of rules/conventions. Furthermore, the direct method mistakenly assumes that teachers and students can establish in a classroom a natural discourse community, where, as we've already seen, structure is indeed acquired unconsciously as language learners, specifically children, engage in communicative acts. Another weakness, certainly, is the emphasis on oral language development. Although students use reading aloud as a way to practice speech and generate discussion, they have little opportunity to develop literacy skills in the target language.

The Natural Approach

Krashen and Terrell (1982) advocate what they call the Natural Approach, which, like the direct method, operates on the assumption that a second language is learned in much the same way as the first language, that is, by unconsciously making connections and identifications among object, action, and word. The learner uses acquired grammatical rules and syntax to monitor speech and to correct errors. This approach necessarily emphasizes the importance of the learning environment because teachers must approximate the interplay of pragmatic factors that lead to first-language acquisition. As Krashen and Terrell tell us, there must be meaningful input for language learning to occur in a natural way, and the oral message must be very clear or it will simply be noise to the language learner.

The Natural Approach has much in its favor, and when it was introduced it offered a significant alternative to the audio-lingual approach that had dominated second-language instruction for years. It seems particularly well suited to younger children who are experiencing their first year of L_2 instruction. It capitalizes on low anxiety and maximum context, is very positive, and serves to enhance students' self-esteem. These affective factors are especially important considerations in the early grades.

We must recognize, however, that various difficulties arise during implementation. For example, teachers may be able to generate a clear message, but they are likely to find it very difficult to create in a classroom that natural environment that characterizes first-language acquisition. Also, discourse monitoring is a crucial part of the method, and teachers are supposed to help students effectively assess their own language production, yet for second-language learners the whole process of monitoring is quite problematic.

Monitoring in this context is the ability to scan one's utterances, detect errors, and make repairs. But how do speakers come to detect a source of trouble in what they are saying? Krashen and Terrell don't really tell us. Yet we know that monitoring and self-repair of one's own discourse is very similar to processing someone else's; it involves a matching procedure to test one message (what was heard) against another (what was meant).

The process must be a conscious one (see Bock, 1982; Foder, 1983; Levelt, 1983). Where attention is lacking we will find those slips of the tongue that go uncorrected because they are undetected. In other words, speakers must deliberately match their utterances against the model formulated by their intentions (which commonly is deemed to exist as inner speech—see Chapter 2). After matching, they must formulate a plan for correction or adjustment, which suggests that speakers must also have enough linguistic competence not only to identify the problem but to correct it.

Although monitoring and self-repair are commonly observed among L_1 speakers, there is some question as to how successfully beginning second-language learners can monitor their discourse when using the target language. In the early stages of their exposure to L_2, their inner speech is likely to be in L_1, making any matching procedure extremely difficult. It is on this level, in fact, that we frequently encounter L_1 interference. If a speaker's native language, for example, lacks articles, the monitoring process would fail to reveal any difficulty in English utterances produced without articles. Moreover, limited lexical, phonological, and syntactic resources will severely restrict planning for corrections.

We recognize the importance of the Natural Approach, even though we are aware of its weaknesses, particularly in regard to addressing the differences that exist between acquiring a first language and learning a second. The difficulty associated with implementation may prevent students from learning to speak accurately, and they may not attain levels of proficiency beyond rudimentary skills (Genesee, 1987). Higgs and Clifford (1982) refer to this problem as "early fossilization" and argue that students need more incentive to succeed than the Natural Approach offers if they are to move to higher levels of proficiency. They also maintain that corrective feedback must be part of any second-language instruction if students are to succeed.

Krashen and Terrell clearly acknowledge the role such feedback must play in helping students develop a monitor, but they make little provision for a cognitive base, that is, any explicit explanation of language's rule-governed nature, in language learning. Their argument is that the brain's innate capacity for language makes such a component unnecessary in the right environment. All students need is appropriate input.

Other Approaches

Over the last few years, several other approaches to second-language instruction have found their way into American schools, but like the direct method and the Natural Approach, they have many features in common. Total physical response, the silent way, and suggestopedia, for example, are all variations of a natural approach to language teaching and learning. Oral communication again is the main goal of each.

Total physical response (TPR) aims at developing receptive language. That is, students are not expected to respond orally until they are comfortable doing so. The emphasis is on developing listening skills. Students listen closely to their teachers, observe their modeling and react to their commands with actions. Based on the observation that much of a child's first-language experience consists of imperatives, teachers will say "walk" and demonstrate it by walking; students are asked to respond not by repeating the word but by actually walking. Later teachers might say "Walk to the window and open it" or "Walk to the door and close it." In each instance, students respond by performing the action.

We would note that much TPR instruction occurs in the classroom under normal circumstances throughout routines of the day, such as lining up for recess and lunch, sitting down and standing up, raising one's hand to ask a question, going to the chalkboard, turning the lights on and off, and so forth. Therefore, we suggest that it would be a mistake to place undue emphasis on imperatives and vocabulary that children are likely to learn anyway by virtue of being in the classroom and watching other children perform routine tasks at the teacher's command.

A problem with this approach is that it may become too classroom-specific and may tend to over-emphasize simple actions that may be learned without much prompting. Greater learning would likely occur if teachers presented less common imperatives and broader vocabulary. Using props to name objects and actions related to history, science, and literature or to places students visit on school trips is an exciting alternative.

The silent way is similar to TPR in the sense that students must pay close attention to the context provided by teachers and must rely on their own deductive powers to connect the meanings of words with the objects and actions they represent. Teachers, however, remain silent. Learning results from students' interaction with materials. The assumption is that language is not the result of habit but of a cognitive process the learners use to discover the rules of language. The four language modes, listening, speaking, reading, and writing, are used from the beginning, each reinforcing the other.

Manipulative materials, such as Cuisenaire (multicolored) rods and charts are used to illustrate the structure of the language. For example, teachers may use a sound-color chart that contains various rods of different colors, each representing a vowel or a consonant sound. By pointing to each rod and saying each sound the rod represents, teachers guide students to learn consonant and vowel sounds of the language. Later, students learn to identify each sound combination with words, then with sentences. They then write the sentences they created. The students use inner criteria they developed on their own to correct their language production.

Suggestopedia, an approach Georgi Lozanov developed in 1978, is based on the idea that students have affective and cognitive blocks that prevent them from mastering a language easily. The focus of the method is therefore on relaxation techniques designed to lower these blocks, the assumption being that relaxation will help students concentrate and retain new vocabulary and structures of the target language.

This method makes use of the environment to free students from interfering thoughts. For example, the teacher will subdue classroom lighting, provide comfortable chairs or bean-bags, and play soothing music, usually of a classical variety. The next step involves certain physiological exercises, such as regulating one's breathing, associated with reaching a relaxed, meditative state. Then the goal is to appeal to student's inner experiences and unconscious minds through suggestion to retain new language learning. Once students are in a suggestible state, the method resembles the audio-lingual approach in that teachers provide oral patterns repeatedly that students rehearse.

There's a certain appeal in the notion that affective blocks contribute to the difficulties of second-language learning. We know, for example, that high anxiety levels can hinder learning, and there is some research that suggests people may be prone to anxiety when asked to engage in any language task that will be monitored or evaluated (Daly & McCroskey, 1984). Moreover, Lozanov develops his rationale for this approach in part on the basis of the extremely popular idea that people use only about 10 percent of their brains; if there were just some way to discover how to use more, it would be possible to open up limitless human potential.

Realistically, however, we have no reason to believe that the relaxation techniques associated with suggestopedia can attenuate students' anxiety or result in a state of mind conducive to learning. Indeed, the approach itself is strikingly similar to hypnosis, which can be used to enhance certain kinds of rote memorization that don't require long-term recall but is essentially useless for complex, creative actions like generating meaningful language (Restak, 1988). Also, since the mid-1970s a wide range of studies has examined the brain at work through the means of advanced scanning devices capable of producing videos of mental processes (see Lassen, Ingvar, & Skinhoj, 1978). They show that even simple mathematical calculations engage large areas of the cortex and that the popular belief that people use only 10 percent of their brains is simply wrong.

"Sheltered English" and ESL

The above methods generally assume some level of bilingualism on the part of the teacher. Yet lack of appropriate personnel often makes it impossible to teach in the native language, and as a result schools are forced to provide subject-area instruction in English. We must stress that trying to teach content material in English to students who aren't proficient in English is undesirable. But in such cases, we commonly find schools have few choices, so they use an approach called "sheltered English," in which a monolingual teacher gives instruction in the content areas.

Students will not be learning new concepts, they will only learn new English structure and vocabulary. New concepts in content areas will have to be taught in the native language. It is possible that with some coordination, students' learning of new concepts would then be used immediately thereafter to teach English vocabulary and sentence structure in the same way that English language and structure were taught through literature. Teachers cannot assume, however, that a sophisticated concept will be learned as a result of using it to teach English as a second language. Some incidental learning is likely to occur, but it is unwise to depend on serendipitous learning to develop academic literacy. There must be purpose and goals in teachers' lesson plans. Therefore, we recommend that known concepts be used as the context for teaching English structure and vocabulary and that the native language be used to teach grade-level content.

Sheltered English is an approach to teach content material via English when it is not possible to use the native language. English as a second language may be taught within the context of a content area, such as literature, social sciences, or math; however, the purpose of the lesson differs. In this regard it is important to distinguish between sheltered English and ESL. The use of the Natural Approach and the emphasis on meaningful context may have enforced the notion that sheltered English can be used in lieu of ESL and that by doing one teachers will have fulfilled their obligation to do the other. As a result, some teachers mistakenly think they have taught English just because they have taught a lesson in social studies, say, using sheltered English. In reality, they have taught social studies, not English. However, if they then extend this lesson to teach English vocabulary that pertains to the community, building and practicing English sentences, they are also teaching ESL.

The purpose in ESL is to teach English-language vocabulary, structure, grammar, and oral communication, within a comprehensible, meaningful context. It is not to teach new content material. Practice given to students to enforce retention of the new learning would deal with vocabulary linguistic issues, not with content per se.

Although there are clear overlaps and obvious interactions in learning, using sheltered English as a ''natural'' approach to ESL rather than as a means of teaching content will result not only in minimal understanding and retention of subject matter but in even lower mastery of English-language skills. The level of preparation for academic literacy will thus be shallow and superficial. We therefore recommend that teachers who find themselves in a sheltered program be aware of the differences that exist between ESL and sheltered English and that they build from each rather than choose to do one in lieu of the other.

Some Conclusions about Methods

With the exception of the grammar-translation method, all the other approaches to second-language instruction we have reviewed focus exclusively on oral proficiency. From this perspective alone, we must conclude that they are inadequate in achieving the pedagogical (as opposed to the sociopolitical) goals of bilingual education. That is, they cannot give second-language learners the literacy skills they need to succeed academically.

Furthermore, the several methods that stress establishing a natural discourse environment assume first-language acquisition and second-language learning are essentially identical. Although we recognize significant merit in the proposal that the two processes have much in common, we must conclude that the stronger claim of identity is highly questionable, particularly in a school setting. In addition, these methods are generally lacking a cognitive base that will overtly help students develop a monitor with which to correct speech and writing toward the norm of native proficiency.

We know, of course, that preschool children removed from their native-language environment and placed in one governed by a different language will begin learning L_2 in essentially the same way they were learning L_1. But we must note that *preschoolers are in the stages of development during which they would have learned any language anyway, using the same processes.*

This phenomenon cannot be readily generalized to older children for whom a different process appears to obtain. That is, unlike preschoolers, older children utilize their knowledge of and experience with their first language to help them master the second. Certainly, the need for meaningful input remains critical, as does the need for context and so forth, but what older children make of such information must necessarily be different from what a two-year-old would make of it (See Bates, 1976; Scardamalia & Bereiter, 1983).

We are not suggesting that the methods we've reviewed will not work—within their fairly well-defined limits and goals, they will. It is these limits, however, that may preclude academic success. Thus, overall, they seem to be lacking in one way or another.

The methods that focus on oral language development, such as the Natural Approach, do so at the expense of literacy and connections with native-language skills for transfer. They also tend to develop only a minimal level of oral language competence. After this minimal level is attained, no component exists to maximize and elevate students to academic literacy.

The grammar-translation method lacks an oral component and therefore is quite inappropriate for modern languages like English. But it does have some worthwhile characteristics. For example, it may include a cognitive base related to English grammar, although too often the potential benefits of this base are offset by reliance on drills and exercises unrelated to natural language production.

TAKING A NEW LOOK AT GRAMMAR-TRANSLATION: A COMPREHENSIVE APPROACH

The goal of helping students become literate in English as well as their native language brings us to ask: Which second-language approach will produce literacy as well as oral proficiency? Our response to this question is to offer an alternative that arises out of the dual goals of literacy and oral proficiency and that draws on some of the methods already discussed. We call it the "Comprehensive Approach" (see Rivers, 1981, for a similar alternative).

At its center is our view of language as a social action and our understanding that bilingual students can achieve literacy in English only if they have opportunities to read and write it. Because reading ability is crucial to everything else students do, we include in the Comprehensive Approach a strong translation component designed to give students significant encounters with texts.

We believe that in learning a second language children make use of what they know in their first language. In other words, the native language has a very active role in assisting second-language learning. To deny that children do not make use of what they know implies that each new learning activity takes place in a void and is ultimately independent. Yet we understand that effective teachers always build on what students already know and encourage connections for future learning (Hunter, 1982). On this account, our approach stresses creating a classroom workshop where students interact with one another as well as with the teacher. It is a student-centered rather than a teacher-centered environment. As such, it is best understood through the kinds of activities students engage in. Some we have already alluded to: having students develop oral essays they then put into writing, having them create stories that are then "published" for the entire class, and so on.

This approach is obviously linked to grammar-translation, which we believe can significantly help language-minority children develop cultural literacy if suitably modified. By carefully selecting literary texts, teachers can introduce students to American values and guide them through works that include the many cultures and ethnic groups that are an integral part of the American historical tradition.

Because the grammar-translation method makes use of students' native language through translation, it facilitates transfer of native-language skills. As students are engaged in making meaning using their native language and English, they make mental connections with what they already know, thereby reinforcing the retention of new information. The second language is enriched by the native language.

In addition, the grammar-translation method requires analyses and interpretations, which involve critical thinking, so it prepares students for higher-level academic skills. With guidance from teachers, it can begin developing critical literacy. When students are presented with a literary text, their teacher's questions about it—such as those related to how the main character's problem developed, how it was resolved, and so on—can enhance the sort of cognitive skills that are part of the school experience.

STRATEGIES FOR PRELITERATE STUDENTS

As we noted in Chapter 4, preliterate students are those who have not yet learned to read and write in either the native or the second language. They may be compound bilinguals, having acquired two languages from birth. If one of them was English, they are likely to be taught in the traditional school curriculum and to pursue native-language literacy as enrichment.

Some preliterates may be older children or even adults, but the situation encountered most often in schools is that preliterates are between five and eight. Moreover, they have attended school only briefly or not at all. They are usually coordinate bilinguals, having acquired the home language and being exposed formally to a new language in school. These are the children for whom bilingual programs were created in the United States, where they are taught to read in their native language.

The teachers' concern in regard to these students will be to introduce English gradually while building native-language literacy skills. The goal should be to develop native literacy not only for its own sake but to provide a foundation of linguistic skills that will later transfer to English. Although initially it's necessary to conceive of these skills as being limited to functional literacy, teachers should never forget that they are laying the foundation for more demanding cultural and critical literacy.

The Comprehensive Approach: Younger Preliterates

The strategies related to the Comprehensive Approach recognize the social nature of language and the importance of building a classroom "community" of language users who interact with one another as they go about learning. They also include activities that require students to practice the four language modes. The range of specific techniques teachers can develop to realize these strategies, however, is quite broad, limited only by the availability of appropriate texts and imagination. Given this range, we will describe a single activity that seems representative and readily generalizable.

With younger preliterates, fairy tales commonly make ideal texts around which to center activities. Teachers should select those that students already know, because prior knowledge will contribute to the meaningfulness of the input as well as reduce anxiety about using English. Both factors will enhance students' comprehension. Suppose the fairy tale is *Little Red Riding Hood*. Even though they don't understand English, students will soon recognize what story is being presented. The language context will be clear, which will allow students to better match the sounds of English to meaning.

Teachers would read the fairy tale in English, using as many illustrations as possible. They should also present the characters using puppets, helping students with vocabulary pertaining to the story, such as *mother, grandmother, girl, wolf, hunter, house, woods*, and so on. The children listen at first, then should help tell the story in a group, chorally, by repeating sentences in English with their teacher.

Involvement is elicited by having students generate connections between the story and their own experiences. For this activity, the native language may be used minimally to allow students to convey their thoughts better, but teachers should translate their comments into English, asking the class to repeat the translation. Teachers can ask students about having grandmothers, whether they ever brought grandmother a gift of food, and what types of food might be in Little Red Riding Hood's basket. They can ask whether students have ever taken a walk in the woods, whether there were woods in their native countries, whether they have ever seen a wolf, what animals they know resemble wolves, and so on. These discussions can take place using the native language as well as English, but teachers should reinforce English vocabulary.

The possibilities for generating vocabulary and discussion are rich. After students have learned a few English words, they can illustrate the main characters of the fairy tale and write down who they are. This activity will provide an introduction to composition. In small groups or as a class, students can retell the story orally using their own words, and teachers can write down their versions using a big chart that enables all students to view the results. In effect, the students recreate the fairy tale, sometimes adding new characters or changing the setting.

Working with fairy tales in this way helps students internalize such concepts as narrative sequencing, main idea, and even cause and effect as they strive to alter the text. The activity also incorporates grade-level curricular skills in language arts while teaching students English. It is student-centered and additive in that the native language is used to negotiate meaning when necessary, and the children's culture is used in either selecting the fairy tale or discussing it.

Literature-based activities are meant to be developed over time. A teaching unit based on one story book, for example, could take a minimum of three to a maximum of six weeks, depending on children's interest and involvement. Once students are used to working with fairy tales and are used to the process and the expectations of their teachers, contextual cues become clearer, which will result in higher comprehension and better retention. Eventually, it will no longer be necessary to use texts that students are familiar with; other literature from the mainstream curriculum will work equally well. Also, teachers can use more English as they help students discuss the texts.

Addressing the Needs of Older Preliterates

Obviously, not all preliterate students will be young children. In some cases they may be 10 or older. Yet the technique outlined above can be adapted to the age and interests of older preliterates by making appropriate adjustments. For example, older students are not likely to find *Little Red Riding Hood* particularly stimulating, so teachers may want to select something with more appeal, such as *Puss 'n Boots, The Princess and the Pea*, or *The Ugly Duckling*. The activities, however, would be quite similar to those described above.

Whatever the age of their students, teachers should be guided by two principles when selecting materials. First, in the initial stages of instruction, students should be familiar with the text, which makes the context of the lessons more meaningful. Second, the purpose for using literature is to teach English.

When using fairy tales with older preliterates, the level of discussion can sometimes become sophisticated. We once used this technique with fifth-grade preliterates and were pleasantly surprised to hear a student comment that the main idea in *Little Red Riding Hood* was the fight between good and evil and that evil was represented by the wolf. Teachers should expect student discussions and analyses to take numerous turns that can be exciting and interesting.

With adult preliterates, teachers can use the same approach, although we recommend that the primary source of content come from students themselves rather than texts. Freire's (1970) pedagogy of "problem posing" will be particularly appropriate for preliterate adults who may also fit into the category of oppressed minority (see also Freire & Macedo, 1987). Students analyze their own reality in terms of conflict resolutions, that is, in terms of problems and how to solve them. The approach is meaningful because it is based on students' daily reality and because it involves consciousness raising (see Graman, 1988, for a possible application of this pedagogy to teaching ESL).

STRATEGIES FOR LITERATE STUDENTS

Literate students have many advantages over preliterate students. They know the relationship between oral language and written texts. They know the mechanics of reading and writing. They are also likely to be older and to have been in school, which means that they will probably possess content-area knowledge commensurate with their grade level. Teachers can use all these advantages as a base to further develop their budding higher-level literacy skills and their oral communication.

The most important element in teaching literate students is transferring skills from their native language to English. What students know about reading and writing in their native language will inform what they do when reading and writing in English. Furthermore, the question of transfer is particularly significant for children who participated in bilingual education programs and are literate in their native language. We will discuss such students in the next chapter.

At this point, our focus is on addressing the needs of newly arrived immigrants who are literate and non- or limited English proficient. The interactive nature of the four language modes will, in our view, allow native-language literacy skills to enhance second-language oral communication skills.

Using the Comprehensive Approach with Literate Students

Language activities using the Comprehensive Approach will begin with texts in the students' native language. These texts can be literature from the students' culture, histories, biographies, work in the social sciences, student-generated material, and so on. In other words the range of possible selections is large, restricted only by the principle of meaningfulness.

A short essay or poem in students' native language is one way to begin. Teachers should tell students in their language that they will be translating the text into English and that they will use it to learn English words and language patterns. After teachers read the text aloud several times, they should encourage students to start repeating the text chorally. The lesson would proceed in much the same way as the fairy tales lesson for preliterates, with teachers using illustrative materials.

Specific activities could include using dictionaries to look up words that are then entered into a vocabulary log, paraphrasing the text, and discussing particular meanings of expressions and/or words. Students can extract verbs and act them out; they can extract adjectives, talk about them, find other similar adjectives, create new sentences using those adjectives, and so on. They can also use the vocabulary they have learned to create new sentences of their own, which they would write, read, and use in short conversations. If the native language uses a script other than Roman, students can start learning the alphabet.

Dialogues, plays, and choral reading are techniques that work well with literate students. After studying a text, students can write and produce plays based on the work. Making props for their oral productions provides a good context for language learning because students will be applying new vocabulary in a purposeful way. Teachers should encourage students to translate back and forth between their native language and English to reinforce vocabulary and language patterns.

As language skills develop, students can begin working with grade-level textbooks as a means of learning more English. They will not be able to proceed in the same way as native English speakers because the intention is to learn the language, not the content. But using grade-level textbooks will serve to motivate students to higher academic achievement, will expose them to the content material in its real school context, and will make clear that teachers' expectations are that they achieve in English at grade level.

Teachers must be careful to separate in their own minds the different goals associated with reading textbooks. For students learning English, it is a mistake to attempt to teach content rather than language skills. Certainly, some incidental content learning may occur, but it will be incidental. If the focus is content material, teachers will have to use the native language.

STRATEGIES FOR POSTLITERATE STUDENTS

As we mentioned in Chapter 4, postliterate students are those who have completed secondary education in their country. They therefore have the broadest knowledge base and the greatest potential for academic success of all the categories we have described.

One risk for these students is that second-language learning may be too superficial and may not be sufficiently challenging. We therefore recommend that teachers use sophisticated materials from which to draw English vocabulary, syntax, and semantics. Starting with translations of literary short stories from students' native culture is one possibility, but it is not as important as it is with the other categories. Older postliterate students will not be suffering from low self-esteem. Of course, in addition to works from the native culture, teachers can use traditional American short stories by authors like Hemingway, Steinbeck, and so on. Because these authors may have been translated into the students' native language, they may already know some of the stories. Nonfiction work offers another source of language as well as information about American history and culture.

When analyzing these works, teachers may want to focus students' attention on language patterns, teaching grammar and meaning in the context of talk about texts. This approach is the opposite of traditional approaches to grammar that stress drills and exercises. The lessons are more meaningful because they are embedded in texts that convey meaning, unlike workbook exercises.

Like literate students, the postliterates would use translations, discussions, and dialogues to practice both oral communication and literacy in English. Given their higher literacy level, it may be desirable to place more emphasis on oral language development than on translations, providing more opportunities for dialogues and discussions.

SETTING THE STAGE FOR INSTRUCTION: ORALITY AND LITERACY

With the above framework, you should recognize that developing a meaningful context for language and literacy emerges as a fundamental requirement for a successful classroom. In our view, literacy is a social phenomenon. On this account, as Frank Smith (1989) says, "Individuals become literate not from the formal instruction they receive, but from what they read and write about and who they read and write with" (p. 355).

In the next two chapters, we will explain how to structure a classroom environment that emphasizes the social nature of reading and writing. By way of preface, we state here that you should not only plan activities that ask students to practice the four language modes of speaking, listening, reading, and writing but should sequence them such that they reinforce one another. We know, for example, that the oral skills among most of our language-minority students will be higher than their literacy skills (Carroll, 1986) and that they can draw on their oral skills to develop literacy. We would therefore suggest that an effective classroom environment will be one that combines orality and literacy. Instruction that utilizes this combination is usually called a "whole-language approach" to teaching.

For writing instruction, Robert Zoellner (1969) outlined a simple method of bringing speech and writing together to enhance students' language skills. He referred to this method as a "talk/write" program. In his analysis, most writing instruction follows a model best described as "think/write." That is, students are asked to think about their essays and then write their texts.

There are numerous difficulties associated with the "think/write" approach. For example, it assumes that students know how to think appropriately about a topic, that they are able to ask themselves the sort of questions that must be asked if one is to get beyond the obvious. Very little evidence exists to support this assumption. It also encourages a false model of writers working in isolation, removed from a specific community, suggesting that when left alone the mind generates significant thoughts that can then be transferred to paper.

The talk/write method, on the other hand, implicitly recognizes the importance of immediate feedback that is a response to ideas that emerge during the drafting stage of writing, and it emphasizes the social nature of language. Moreover, it recognizes the fact that speech is the primary mode of expression for our students. Thus, in Zoellner's method, students develop an "oral essay" for the teacher, who offers feedback and advice.

Producing the essay orally has the effect of creating a pre-text that is more fully elaborated than what results from simply thinking about a topic, because the presence of the teacher provides a meaningful context and an audience that will not accept skeletally thin discourse. When using the think/write approach, a student may be satisfied with a vague or sketchy pre-text, but when speaking before the teacher, it is understood that more is expected.

Zoellner argues that the talk/write method allows students to take advantage of their existing rhetorical and linguistic competence. We would also add that it can give students a sense of having completed a composition before they start writing, which has the effect of making the writing process itself largely an act of revision. Both factors lead to improved performance. The success of this method may be linked to the fact that thinking/writing fails to provide the linguistic and rhetorical reinforcement inherent in thinking/speaking/writing.

The biggest difficulty you would face in using this method is the time constraint that teachers must contend with. Meeting with every student for ten minutes, for example, would require five hours for a class of 30. Faced with this reality, many teachers utilize work groups in which individual students talk through their writing projects before starting them, while the other members listen. At the end of each "talk," the group discusses the project and offers suggestions for development. In this setting, the teacher works his or her way around the groups, pausing to listen and offer advice as needed. This environment offers the advantages inherent in the talk/write model but avoids the difficulty presented by trying the meet with every student before a task begins. Chapter 7 explores this environment in detail.

CONCLUSION

This chapter examined the more widely used methods for second-language teaching. These methods can be divided into two categories: on the one hand are those that focus exclusively on literacy, and on the other are those that concentrate primarily on oral proficiency. Neither category in itself is complete, and the methods that are associated with each will not help students attain the goal of academic success.

We therefore proposed the Comprehensive Approach as a means of incorporating the four language modes while using the native language to transfer skills in a cognitive way. The essence of the Comprehensive Approach is its balance of oral proficiency and literacy in a student-centered environment. It draws on the notion that language (and therefore literacy) is a social action and that bilingual students can achieve literacy in English only if they have opportunities to read and write it. The Comprehensive Approach makes use of students' native language through translation activities.

The chapter then examined ways to use the Comprehensive Approach with preliterate, literate, and postliterate students. Fairy tales, for example, provide an effective means of introducing younger students to a range of activities that can enhance literacy.

CHAPTER 7

Teaching Reading

OVERVIEW

In the previous chapter, we proposed a comprehensive approach to teaching oral language communication and literacy skills to students in language programs. This approach is predicated on the assumption that all four modes of language—reading, listening, speaking, and writing—are interrelated and that students make use of their native language to become orally competent and literate in a second language. Therefore, the strategies we suggested integrated all four language skills. In this chapter we deal specifically with reading instruction and refine how teachers can use the Comprehensive Approach.

It is extremely important to keep in mind the student population for whom instruction is intended. Students will have various language competencies and literacy levels in one or more languages when they enroll in school. Schools are therefore obliged to properly assess students' competencies in both the native and the second language. Such assessment helps determine what kind of instructional program would be best for individual students, and it is central to student placement. For these reasons, we pay special attention in this chapter to the reclassification of students who began in bilingual programs as LEP and learned to read in the native language with the intention of shifting to an English-only program. Admittedly, the length of native-language reading instruction has been and continues to be controversial. Yet its importance cannot be underestimated if we wish to accomplish the goal of literacy as well as academic achievement.

Consistent with our discussion of literacy in chapters 1 and 2, we review three theoretically sound approaches used to teach reading: the language experience approach (LEA), the core literature approach, and the reading-while-listening approach. We examine in detail how they can be used with language-minority students. We offer specific techniques for teaching reading to the categories of students we defined earlier—preliterate, literate, and postliterate—keeping in mind that these categories refer to native-language literacy and taking into account the students' language proficiency in English.

READING IN THE NATIVE LANGUAGE AND RECLASSIFICATION

As we noted in Chapter 3, students who upon enrollment are classified as LEP and assigned to a bilingual program begin to read in their native language while they learn English as a second language. For these students the issue of reclassification is extremely important.

In regard to reading instruction, reclassification means that there is a point at which these students are considered to be *Functional English Proficient* (FEP). After reclassification, they are no longer eligible to receive reading instruction in their native language.

As you can imagine, this issue tends to be highly controversial for the ideological reasons we discussed in Chapter 4. The central question is: How long should one teach reading in the native language before discontinuing it in favor of reading in English? Those who subscribe to the belief that more English instruction will produce more English proficiency tend to answer this question with the statement: As short a time as possible.

Our position, consistent with several other scholars (see Cummins, 1988; Toukomaa & Skutnabb-Kangas, 1977; Snipper, 1985), is that students should continue reading in their native language until they have achieved a functional level of literacy, which we have already defined as the fourth-grade reading level. We aren't suggesting, certainly, that instruction in English should not take place until the fourth grade. Such a misconception leads some people to fear that students will be "held back" in bilingual programs and will never learn English. It stems from a compensatory view of bilingual education that is by definition supposed to compensate for the students' "deficiency." Given the research on language transferability and the weaknesses of the language-deficit model, it seems clear that any time spent on native-language instruction will enrich second-language knowledge. Enriching programs are far more likely to attain positive literacy outcomes.

The fact that students will be reading in their native language does not preclude participation in instruction to promote English language proficiency. The two processes are not contradictory; they complement each other, given the interrelationship among languages. Instruction in both native-language reading and ESL can happen simultaneously, in a parallel way, throughout the school day.

Students can be taught ESL for a certain block of time, content-area material for another block of time, reading in the native language at another time, reading in English at still another time. Scheduling, grouping and regrouping students, teaming, and planning in advance on the part of the teachers will allow students to receive appropriate instruction.

We realize that a four-year reading program in the native language will place a heavy financial burden on a school district. Yet it is a question of priorities. If a longer native-language reading program will produce more literate and academically successful students, as research indicates, any money will be well spent. The funds will not have to go for compensatory and remedial programs when students fail for lack of a strong literacy background in the native language. The focus, therefore, is on prevention, not remediation.

READING METHODS: CREATING A CONTEXT FOR READING

If we were to identify the single most important contribution literacy research has made to teaching over the last dozen years, it would be that language learning must take place in a meaningful context. Our discussion of phonics and sight vocabulary in Chapter 2 described two approaches that fail to take context into account, and we criticized them accordingly. At this point, we want to describe two approaches that do contextualize reading and a third that does not but that nevertheless may prove useful in teaching reading in a bilingual classroom.

The Language Experience Approach

The language experience approach (LEA) is based on the observation that children remember best what is most meaningful to them and what they themselves have generated. It therefore focuses on developing reading materials from things students have to say, whether they be invented stories or narrative accounts of events.

Teachers using this approach, for example, might take advantage of a field trip students experienced and have them produce a group or an individual story about it. Younger children can dictate the story to the teacher, who will write it down. Older students can write their own. These stories are then read by the children, forming their reading text. With this approach, eventually children should be able to read a library book at their grade level.

In the case of students who have access to word processors, they may type their stories and output them on a printer. In fact, IBM has offered for several years computer work stations that are designed to allow kindergarten and first-grade students to generate their own stories, publish them on printers, and share them with the rest of the class. The program is called *Writing to Read*, and numerous reports suggest it is quite successful (see J. D. Williams, 1989, for a brief review).

Often teachers of younger students will transcribe stories into Big Books that the children illustrate. They then gather around and read their stories aloud. Students generally are more motivated to read their own work when they are sharing it with others, and these activities reinforce the social nature of discourse on all levels.

Older students can engage in a similar activity by binding their work into a book that can be photocopied in sufficient quantity to allow them to take one home to share with family and friends. By working with other teachers, it's possible to arrange for book exchanges that allow students to share stories and ideas with their counterparts in other classes.

Although the language experience approach most commonly involves narratives and poetry, it can also be used with exposition and with content-area activities. Students in social studies, for example, can explain the period of America's westward expansion chronologically, with members of the class divided into groups, working with different periods. When they publish their book, they will have a coherent "history" that they can share among themselves and with others. Or when presenting a historical period, you can ask students to take on the roles of people who lived during that period and have them produce representative texts. These might include newspaper articles for a collaborative activity, or letters designed to be shared with their historical friends.

These techniques are much less structured than what is typically associated with basal readers. They require a measure of skill, because teachers must draw new stories and vocabulary from students and provide the practice necessary for students to remember words. A criticism of this method is that students may not progress as much as they should if the teacher is inexperienced, but such is the case with just about any method. Another criticism is that students may not be able to transfer from reading their stories to reading an actual book, but to date no reliable data exist to substantiate this argument.

The Core Literature Approach

The rationale for this approach develops out of the belief that students need to experience models of professional writing. This need is linked to the idea that such models are related to improved language performance, especially in writing, and to the idea that they serve as important sources of cultural information. Like the LEA, it is based on the assumption that children learn to read by reading, but its advocates argue that children need an actual book to become literate. In many ways, the core literature approach may be viewed as a reaction not only to phonics instruction but to basal readers as well as the LEA, because it implies that a significant purpose of reading is to enjoy good literature. The goal, as in the LEA, is to provide students with reading materials that are both meaningful and interesting, but the source of meaning and interest is quite different—it is outer-directed rather than inner-directed.

The core literature approach also differs from the LEA in that it more actively endorses teaching phonetic skills and sight vocabulary as comprehension tools within the context of the story. The approach has been moved from the particular to the general. That is, rather than beginning with letter recognition and decoding out of context and allowing the students to have books to read only after they have mastered all the sound symbols, children begin with the actual purpose for reading—a story they can enjoy and relate to. From there they learn specific skills, without losing sight of the general purpose for learning to read— to enjoy good literature.

Core literature, as the name implies, emphasizes a core of texts supposedly representative of the American experience. The connection with cultural literacy is significant. In California, for example, the State Department of Education has recommended a list of literature texts the districts may choose from for use at each grade level. The list includes children's books, fairy tale, novels like Steinbeck's *The Red Pony*, and books written by members of various ethnic groups or about those groups.

Students begin in kindergarten by reading from books like *The Little Engine that Could* or *The Three Bears*. In the third grade they might read *Charlotte's Web* or *Charlie and the Chocolate Factory*; in the sixth grade they might read *James and the Giant Peach* or *Annie and the Old One*. The list is extensive, so teachers have a great deal of freedom to choose texts that will match the specific characteristics of students in their schools. All students receive their own copy of the books and engage in a range of language activities that relate to their reading.

It is important to select books carefully not only for content and reading level but for vocabulary. We recommend that teachers strive to use books with a significant number of representational words (nouns, verbs, adjectives, and adverbs) in common. Reading research indicates that students become better readers when their texts have vocabulary that repeats. Rashotte and Torgesen (1985), for example, found that when students read the same words several times in different stories, their reading rate increases.

The reading-related activities teachers provide for students are central in making the core literature approach context-centered. Reading by itself does not make the act of reading meaningful, although certainly we can expect students to find a text like *The Red Pony* more meaningful than a basal reader. Nor does assigning a piece of literature guarantee students will find it enjoyable or interesting. What teachers and students do with their reading is the key to successfully translating this approach into a means of enhancing reading performance and enjoyment.

Certainly, if texts are presented as having problems to solve, teachers can better stress both the social and the personal aspects of making meaning. This process would help move students from functional literacy toward cultural and critical literature. We would also suggest, however, that writing activities are another important means of improving students' language skills. Asking students to analyze their reading may not be appropriate in the core literature approach, because it leads to a mind-numbing dullness that can turn students off and make them resent their texts. But using writing to "play" with the texts seems very worthwhile. Students can introduce new characters into novels or change endings. With texts related to historical events, they can engage in role-playing and write documents such as letters, newspaper articles, and diaries from a historical period. In every case, teachers should aim to help students discover how their own lives are reflected, in one way or another, in the literature they read. This discovery will lead to learning from their reading, and they will enjoy the experience as well.

The Reading-While-Listening Approach

Carol Chomsky (1976), recognizing that reading rate is a significant factor in comprehension, proposed that students could improve their skills by combining texts and audiotapes of the texts. In this procedure, students listen to a tape of a text while they follow along in their books. Using a limited number of texts, students work through them repeatedly until they almost reach the point of memorization. The tape sets the pace of the reading, and for language-minority students it would serve not only as a pronunciation aid but as a model for fluent reading in English. The text reinforces vocabulary and helps develop perceptual skills related to language processing.

After her students had gone through the stories several times, Chomsky worked with them to analyze the main points and to practice vocabulary items. In her study, she reports substantial gains in word recognition skills, comprehension, reading rate, and motivation to read. Since this initial report, several other investigators have achieved similar results (Carbo, 1978; Gamby, 1983).

This approach appears to offer several important advantages in the bilingual classroom, but we would suggest that its effectiveness can be enhanced by having students read aloud along with the tape rather than simply following the words. Reading aloud enables teachers to monitor student progress. Because their English skills are still developing, students are likely to find reading slow and laborious, which detracts significantly from any enjoyment they might experience otherwise. This situation is especially problematic for students who have learned to read in their native language, because the difficulty involved in comprehending English texts may affect their motivation to read and is likely to taint their perception of English and their willingness to master English. The reading-while-listening approach, however, attenuates these difficulties and indeed seems to affect motivation positively (Reitsma, 1988).

Focusing on Comprehension

If you decide to use one of these methods for teaching your students to read in English, keep in mind that your goal is to help them understand and enjoy texts. With this point as a guide, we would recommend that you always follow your reading activity by asking students to identify the main idea of the text. This recommendation follows from our discussion of a top-down approach to reading that focuses on comprehension rather than on word or phoneme recognition. You should note in this regard that recent research suggests that basal readers, because they are highly contrived and don't reflect naturally occurring texts, seem to interfere with students' ability to identify main ideas (Hare, Rabinowitz & Schieble, 1989). Such findings reinforce our perception that basal readers, as well as bottom-up approaches, are not conducive to developing reading ability.

TEACHING READING
TO PRELITERATE STUDENTS

As we noted in Chapter 4, preliterate students are those who have not yet learned to read and write in either the native or the second language. In most cases, such students will be between five and eight years old, although occasionally they may be older. If they have attended school before, they didn't do so long enough to develop any literacy skills. Specifically, there are two types of preliterate students we will be concerned with: those who are non- or limited English proficient and those who are proficient in English.

Teachers will be most concerned with non- or limited English proficient preliterates. Preliterate students who do not speak English proficiently should begin to read in their native language, and they should continue systematically until they have reached the fourth-grade level. As we mentioned earlier, they will not be precluded from learning English. Nor will they be precluded from exposure to the printed word in English. At this point, the goal is to teach reading in the native language and at the same time to prepare students for English-language literacy by incorporating the printed word as part of English-language instruction.

In Chapter 5, we recommended using literature, such as fairy tales, to teach oral communication in English because it helps establish a clear and comprehensible context. Some of the described activities incorporated reading and writing tasks. After the children have engaged in discussions about the story or fairy tale the teacher has told, they can begin retelling it in English, creating their own group story the teacher will copy on a large chart that everyone can see clearly. By the time they get to retelling the story, they are likely to have it memorized, so they will not have any problem recalling particular words or "reading" entire sentences.

Remember that these students will be reading in their native language at some other time during the day. The reading experience in English is only an integrated extension of ESL. At this stage, more time should be spent teaching reading in the native language and teaching English-language development in an integrated approach than teaching reading in English. The time spent on English reading, however, should gradually increase as children move up grade levels.

If this approach is used systematically in a dual-language reading program, by the time the children are in fourth grade they may already be on grade level in English reading. It is when English-language instruction and reading are not linked systematically that children remain several grade levels behind.

Addressing the Needs of Older Preliterates

In some cases, preliterate students may be 10 or older. The approach we illustrated above can be adapted to the age and interest level of the students by utilizing the principles and assumptions on which it is based. For example, for the 10-year-old preliterate, *Little Red Riding Hood* may be not appropriate. Nevertheless, there is still merit in using fairy tales for this age group, provided they are sufficiently mature to capture students' interest. Stories like *Snow White* and *The Ugly Duckling* deal with significant, human issues that are universal, yet the childlike characters are very appealing to young people.

As with younger students, teachers will want to begin by selecting a tale that the class is already familiar with. The procedure for introducing the text and discussing it is identical to the one in the previous section, although teachers will have to judge how appropriate puppets will be for a given class.

We would add a note of caution at this point, however. Older students are likely to become quite involved in the interaction and discussion, and teachers may find themselves encouraging the class to analyze the story simply for the sake of analyzing it. When this happens, there is a tendency to use the native language exclusively, although the purpose of the activity is to build English skills. Teachers shouldn't let their enthusiasm for student interaction move them off task. Bring the discussion back to learning English, in a positive way, by using oral translations and building on students' statements.

TEACHING READING IN ENGLISH
TO LITERATE STUDENTS

In our definition, literate students are those who can read and write in their native language at the fourth-grade level. These students may be new arrivals to the United States, or they may be students who began school lacking English proficiency but who through participation in an appropriate bilingual program learned to read and write in their native language. Their oral language proficiency in English will vary. New arrivals probably will speak no English; the reclassified LEP students may or may not have oral proficiency.

Literate students have many advantages over preliterate students. They know the relationship between oral language and written text. They know the mechanics of reading and writing. They are also likely to be older and to have been in school long enough to have developed commensurate grade-level knowledge of the curriculum. Teachers can use these advantages to build academic literacy and oral communication skills.

As we noted in our discussion of preliterate students, there is a wide range of materials you can use to begin developing English skills. The key is to start with a text in the students' native language. It can be a piece of literature written by a native author, history, social sciences, or texts students have written. Using texts students have produced can be especially worthwhile because it helps make their work with language both more immediate and more meaningful.

After selecting a text, teachers should use the students' native language to let the class know they will be translating passages into English with the aim of learning about the language. Understandably, if teachers aren't proficient in the students' language, they will have to rely on an aide to serve as translator. The lesson then proceeds in the same fashion as already described, with the use of illustrations and props to help convey meaning.

For those students literate in languages that use a non-Roman alphabet, such as Arabic, Farsi, Armenian, Chinese, and so forth, we suggest that the Roman script be presented immediately, incorporated within the Comprehensive Approach. That is, students should practice writing and reading words that arise out of the class discussions of the texts they are using. The reading practice should of course be aloud so teachers can help students with pronunciation.

Students can also retell the text in different ways and with different words. They can discuss the meaning of certain words and their synonyms, can extract vocabulary words to record in their personal word book. They can extract verbs and act them out, and they can extract adjectives, talk about them, find other similar adjectives, create new sentences using those adjectives, and record them in their word book. Finally, they can use the vocabulary they have learned to create new sentences of their own, which they would write, read, and say out loud. Again, all four language modes, listening, speaking, reading, and writing would be used at the same time.

As a culmination for each unit of study, students can write and produce plays, based, for example, on their reading. Although teachers may be tempted to limit this activity to literature, there is no need to do so. History, art, science—indeed the whole curriculum can be dramatized if students are willing to participate. A unit on the space shuttle, for example, could easily lead to an entertaining dramatization of astronauts on a mission.

Making props and writing dialogue for their productions provides a good context for language learning, because students will have a real purpose for using

English. Don't hesitate to translate freely back and forth between the native language and English, because such translation will help students build their vocabulary in both L_1 and L_2 and will also help provide a cognitive base.

As students progress using this approach and as they feel comfortable dealing with English, they can begin working with grade-level textbooks. Clearly, they would not be able to proceed in the same way as native English speakers, because the intent is to learn English vocabulary and structure for communication. But using grade-level texts will motivate them to higher academic achievement, will expose them to the content material in its "real" school context, and will make clear that expectations are that they achieve in English at grade level.

As with preliterate students, teachers cannot assume that literate students will learn content material through a lesson that is planned to teach English-language skills. Again, some incidental learning will occur, but it will not be sufficient. For content-material learning, teachers will have to use the native language. If teachers are monolingual, they will have to do team teaching or work with an aide. We discuss how to do both in Chapter 8.

Students coming from bilingual programs are at a very crucial point, because they have to transfer all the literacy knowledge they have in their native language to be on grade level in English. For these students this point will probably coincide with their reclassification and termination of instruction in the native language.

It isn't likely that they will be able to transfer all their native-language skills to English in one year, especially if they have not been prepared beforehand. Their English communicative and academic language skills should be commensurate with those of the native language for a smooth transition, which requires a systematic language program designed for the range of possible literacy levels.

TEACHING READING IN ENGLISH TO POSTLITERATE STUDENTS

Postliterate students are those who have completed secondary education in their country. They are older than elementary age students, ranging from high school to college age. These students have the broadest content knowledge and the most potential for academic success.

One risk for these students is that second-language learning may be too superficial and not offer enough challenge or content. They will have a high level of literacy in their native language, which can be used to advantage. One way to begin working with these students is to have them perform translations of short stories from their culture, but their high self-esteem and their native-language education do not make this approach crucial to success. It is therefore possible to have students work with American texts that have been translated into their native language. The goal is this instance is twofold: to give students practice that will develop English skills, and to introduce them to reflections of American culture.

A large body of research indicates the uselessness of grammar instruction that is not immediately related to reading or writing tasks (see Hillocks, 1986, for a review). As a result, we urge you to avoid anything that resembles a grammar exercise. Nevertheless, grammar forms a cognitive base that can aid second-language comprehension and production. We therefore suggest that explanations of grammar be intimately linked to the task at hand and that they be incidental to the activity itself. For example, if your students are writing a translation of a text on some aspect of American history, you may observe that several are having difficulty with prepositions. Rather than giving them a set of exercises on prepositions that would be highly decontextualized, you would stop the translation and at that moment give a brief (10 minutes, maximum) explanation of English prepositions. You would then let the students return to their translation and by monitoring them as they work help them implement the grammar lesson.

The focus of teaching reading to postliterate students should be on building on and making connections with the native-language literacy skills they possess. Again all four language modes should be integrated in the reading process, give students the opportunity to use English for oral communication with their peers in class and writing to ensure literacy development.

CONCLUSION

In this chapter, we focused on reading instruction for students who are preliterate, literate, or postliterate. We reviewed three theoretically sound approaches to teaching reading and discussed how they may be used with students who are bilingual or LEP. We recommended strategies within a comprehensive approach.

Moreover, we emphasized the importance of student assessment in capitalizing on students' knowledge in the native language and in finding out their English-language proficiency level. This latter point is particularly important for literate students who may have participated in bilingual education programs. We redefined the concept of transfer, describing it as a continuous process of making connections between the native and second language of each new skill learned. In our view, it is not simply the point of shift from one language of instruction to another. For preliterate students starting out in bilingual programs, we recommended the native-language reading instruction be carried out parallel to instruction in English, until students are literate in their native language.

It isn't unusual for teachers of language-minority students to focus on simple decoding skills when working on reading. Such skills are easier to present, they are commonly linked to workbooks that keep students busy, and they appear very task oriented. In the final analysis, however, such an approach seems antithetical to what we know about how people process language. If their goal is to help students understand their texts, teachers will have to adopt methods of teaching reading that establish a meaningful context for comprehension to take place.

The Comprehensive Approach we have outlined develops such a context. It also encourages a wide range of activities that involve students in listening, speaking, and writing, as well as reading. Limitations of space forced us to describe only one type of text—the fairy tale—that teachers can use in the classroom, but in reality, teachers will be limited only by the native-language experiences of their students. Science texts, history texts, even art texts are appropriate, as long as they match what a class already knows.

CHAPTER 8

Teaching Writing

OVERVIEW

Throughout this text we have emphasized the social nature of language. In Chapter 5, for example, we discussed the "talk/write" approach to teaching writing as an effective way to provide a meaningful context for composing. The following chapter, focusing on students reclassified as English proficient, offers a detailed analysis of how to develop a classroom environment that takes advantage of the benefits inherent in interactive learning. It describes a student-centered structure that evolves out of a workshop approach to instruction.

A significant part of the classroom workshop is peer work groups that provide meaningful input as students develop the initial drafts of an assignment. Students read one another's papers in their groups, offering comments and suggestions for revision. Sometimes they may work on projects together as a team, practicing the collaboration that we find so frequently in natural writing situations.

Several pedagogical benefits have been linked to this sort of classroom environment. First, students accept more responsibility for their success and achievement, because they are more in control of their work. Work groups also encourage cooperative problem solving that can enhance critical-thinking skills, which may be particularly important in mastering L_2 academic literacy. On a more pragmatic level, having students work in class allows teachers to move freely about the room to offer advice on papers that are still in draft form. Students can use this advice immediately to improve their work, modifying language behavior during the composing process, when it is most beneficial.

Our approach to writing instruction for bilingual students is quite different from traditional methods, which emphasize drills and exercises that are supposed to make better writers through teaching standard grammar and usage. In the traditional approach, students write very little, and what writing they do is often limited to sentences and paragraphs. Only occasionally do they write whole essays.

Research in composition studies over the last dozen years suggests that the traditional approach is not particularly effective, that if students are going to improve their writing skill they must have opportunities to write. Moreover, as our discussion of language and literacy acquisition in Chapter 2 suggests, students will need frequent and immediate feedback when writing if they are to expand their repertoire of skills.

THE CLASSROOM AS WORKSHOP

In the context of language acquisition, we consider meaningful input to be functional language directed toward the child, from which he or she derives the underlying grammatical and pragmatic principles that govern language. Teachers who hope to draw on this aspect of acquisition will structure a classroom environment that has similar characteristics. It will be an environment that allows for collaborative learning activities. It will draw on what students already know about discourse, building new skills on old ones by connecting speech, writing, and reading in L_1 with speech, writing, and reading in L_2. It will provide students with frequent opportunities to interact with one another through writing and talking about their writing. And it will allow the teacher to intervene as students are composing, offering advice that can be immediately applied to the task at hand.

In most respects, this view of the classroom is contrary to what we frequently find in schools. It isn't uncommon for teachers to believe bilingual students need special treatment in writing classes. Too often such treatment turns out to be not so special at all, consisting simply of grammar drills and exercises that have nothing to do with producing texts. A wide range of research demonstrates convincingly that grammar instruction doesn't help students write better (see Hillocks, 1986; J. D. Williams, 1989, for a review).

We would argue that when you are teaching writing you are dealing with universals of competence, performance, learning, and acquisition that transcend individual language differences. For example, research over the last few years suggests that nonmainstream students work through writing tasks in about the same way that mainstream students do (Zamel, 1983). Nonnative English speakers use strategies that are essentially identical to those mainstream students use. They develop a pre-text for the discourse that includes both rhetorical features and surface features. When they write, they engage in pausing episodes indicative of mental revisions of the pre-text, just as mainstream students do. They revise recursively, modifying their discourse plans as they go along. Moreover, we find that planning and revising skills in L_1 transfer to L_2 (Jones & Tetroe, 1983).

Congruent with the idea of universals, bilinguals use writing to get things done at the community level, and they use it on the personal level to clarify their thoughts on subjects. It functions, in other words, as a way of knowing. In both cases bilingual writers must also act as effective readers if they are to match their intentions with their output. Through reading and matching, they engage in what Ann Raimes (1985, 1986), suggests is a form of "negotiation" that involves compromises to produce an approximation of intentions.

Negotiation, however, involves risk taking, and many of our bilingual students are likely to be risk adverse. As we saw in Chapter 2, students who have experienced a classroom environment that stresses error correction may be very anxious about language. One of your goals must therefore be to create a learning environment that reduces student anxiety and encourages risk taking.

The writing workshop is fundamental to establishing such a classroom environment. In workshops, students write drafts of assignments and interact with one another while doing so. Students revise drafts and are free to talk and move about the room as they share their writing. They are allowed to assume a great deal of responsibility for their own learning, which means that not everyone will be doing the same thing. Some students may be working alone writing a draft, some may be discussing ways to improve a student's paper, and some may be getting advice from the teacher.

Writing workshops normally are noisy and a bit hectic, which prompts many people to assume that they are unstructured. We would stress, however, that there is an abundance of structure. In our experience, a successful workshop involves not only more structure but more planning than a traditional classroom, because students must be kept busy as well as focused while simultaneously feeling as though they are largely in control of what they are doing. This approach asks teachers to give up much of their tangible control over the minute details of students' behavior to focus on broader aspects of learning. Reducing tangible control commonly demands an accompanying increase in structure, or *in*tangible control.

One of the more effective means of reaching this goal is to have students work through several activities during the course of a lesson. For example, you may spend 15 minutes analyzing a writing sample at the beginning of the hour, 25 minutes writing or rewriting, and then the final 10 minutes letting students talk about the work they have just finished. Or you may use the first 15 minutes having students engage in role-playing to enhance audience awareness, with the remainder of the hour devoted to writing and rewriting. No matter how you structure your lesson, be certain to include some writing as part of every day's activity.

Dealing with Errors

Admittedly, many teachers are reluctant to use a workshop approach to writing instruction with nonnative English speakers. The sorts of errors we find in their writing would seem to suggest that working on the subskills of inflections, subject/verb agreement, and so forth must be our first priority, so there's a strong temptation to turn to drills and exercises to reduce first-language interference.

Although we must certainly help students master the formal conventions of written English, focusing on surface features is wrongheaded for several reasons. Any subskills approach is by definition bottom-up rather than top-down. As we saw in Chapter 2, language processing generally just doesn't utilize bottom-up processes, so it necessarily will be artificial. In addition, the sorts of surface errors we find in students' work are usually unrelated to the broader rhetorical and intellectual skills at the heart of good writing. For example, most people would prefer a thoughtful, interesting paper that has some annoying surface problems to a mechanically flawless paper that has nothing worthwhile to say.

The case against drills and exercises has been made stronger by research suggesting that few of the errors nonmainstream writers make are the result of primary language interference. After collecting and analyzing samples of speech and writing from a group of Spanish/English bilingual children during their first three years of elementary school, Edelsky (1986) reports not only few instances of L_1 interference but few instances of switching between L_1 and L_2.

She concludes that most of the switching she found was "like slips of the pen" and that it decreased significantly by the time children were in the third grade (p. 152). Instances of interference, therefore, appeared to be developmental in nature, eliminated after the children had made greater gains in English proficiency. Her data are congruent with Steve Krashen's (1980) argument that bilingual learners fall back on and use what they know about their first language to fill in linguistic gaps they have in their second. In other words, they use skills they already in L_1 until they acquire the rule in L_2 (also see Calkins, 1983; Dyson, 1982, 1983; Ferreiro & Teberosky, 1982).

If we are going to approach writing instruction from a rhetorical rather than a subskills perspective, we will address students' writing errors as they make them, not through a series of exercises that have no relationship to writing. Edelsky (1986) advocates this approach when she calls for a new way of teaching bilingual students how to write. She calls for an approach that will link reading and writing in a top-down, functional manner, an approach that will view writing as a social action, not as a set of separate subskills.

WRITING AS A COLLABORATION

It's widely believed that writing takes place in a vacuum. As a culture we accept the image of the writer working in lonely isolation, removed from the distractions of the everyday world. In reality, nearly all writing benefits from the advice, suggestions, and editing of a network of friends, colleagues, and supervisors. Writing is fundamentally a public action, and with few exceptions it is fundamentally a collaborative effort.

Bringing this reality into the classroom is an important part of writing instruction for bilingual students. But before it can be implemented, students must get to know one another as well as possible; they must come to think of the class as a group of friends who can be counted on for help and support. Establishing this sense of community involves giving students time to learn about one another. An approach that works well for some teachers involves pairing students off and asking them to interview each other, discovering as much personal information as possible. They then use the interviews as introductions to the whole class. With the idea of bonding in mind, many more teachers simply designate the beginning 20 minutes of the class as "get acquainted time." Students are free to move about the room and free to talk with whomever they wish.

The educational benefits of work groups have been fairly well documented. For example, the cooperation required in group activities appears to lead students to work harder and to discover more than they do when tasks are performed on an individual, competitive basis (Crawford & Haaland, 1972). Genesse (1987) suggests that nonmainstream students often have a learning style that is more compatible with collaborative group work than with competitive, individual efforts.

In addition, work in groups seems to have a positive effect on motivation. Students who aren't strongly motivated to perform will be encouraged by those who are, and for all students the level of motivation seems to remain higher when participating in group work (see Garibaldi, 1979; Gunderson & Johnson, 1980; Johnson & Ahlgren, 1976). In mixed classes, with both mainstream and nonnative English speakers, cooperative work groups provide an effective environment for interaction, potentially enhancing the language/literacy skills of both groups (see Johnson, Johnson & Maruyama, 1983).

Nonnative English-speaking writers characteristically view revision both as an exercise in correcting surface errors and as a signal that they have failed. This perception is especially pervasive among younger students, who typically will not revise on their own (Scardamalia and Bereiter, 1983). The work group, however, alters the nature of writing activities, even for very young children. Multiple drafts are built into each assignment. Students know they are expected to write a draft, share it with others to get feedback, incorporate the feedback into a new draft, and so on, until the paper is finally due. This process alleviates any sense of failure associated with revision.

Organizing Work Groups

Let's consider some of the steps involved in setting up work groups in class. After students have had time to get acquainted, you will need an idea of the range of student writing abilities. An in-class writing task is the accepted way to collect a sample for evaluation. You should emphasize that the essays won't be graded, because class anxiety may be high.

Typically, some students will have richer experiences to draw on than others, which is likely to put less fortunate students at a disadvantage. To ensure a more equitable assignment, you may want to consider making this initial writing task one that is "text based," meaning that it will involve having students read a short passage that they will address in their writing. They need not engage in analyzing the passage itself, but it will be relevant to their writing; it will form the background for the response.

Although many teachers believe this initial writing task provides an accurate measure of students' skills, we would argue the contrary. It works merely as a rough guide in forming work groups. In fact, after many years of teaching, our experience has been that students who perform poorly on this task often turn out to be strong writers and vice versa.

You should be aware that the size of a group is important for effective functioning. In groups of 3, 2 members often take sides against the third. Moreover, in a class of 30, you will have so many groups scattered about that moving among them will be quite difficult. In groups of 4, the members may split evenly whenever they need to make a decision, rendering them ineffective. Five therefore seems to be the ideal number because it avoids the above difficulties and allows for better interaction among members (see Huff & Kline, 1987).

Before groups can function effectively, students must go through a bonding process that unites them in a common purpose. Once the bonding is complete, the group will work as a collaborative unit. In fact, bonding is so crucial to organizing an effective workshop environment that you will need to keep groups together the *entire term* to preserve it. Moving students from group to group may appear to offer more variety in responses to drafts, but the advantage of variety is significantly offset by the breakdown in bonding that results from shifting students around (Huff & Kline, 1987).

We advise against letting students form their own groups; too often the result is a small circle of friends who cannot work well together because they are unable to be candid evaluators of one another's writing. Also, some students may group themselves by gender or, in mixed classes, by races or language. None of these membership patterns is desirable. If at all possible, avoid situations where group members are primarily strong writers or weak writers. Balancing the groups in terms of skill will enable stronger writers to help weaker ones.

Students should arrange their seats into small circles that make it easier for them to work together. Always try to have an empty desk or two separating the groups, if at all possible. Such separation not only leads to a greater sense of bonding within each group but also creates a sense of privacy. Both are important.

Further Benefits of Work Groups

Throughout this text, we have stressed that in a natural setting an individual language user influences and is influenced by his or her immediate discourse community. Work groups offer the best approximation of a natural setting, providing both a sense of empowerment and a community of academic discourse users.

Indeed, it seems difficult to underestimate the importance of peer interaction in a positive learning environment. David Johnson (1980) tells us that such interaction contributes significantly to "internalization of values, acquisition of perspective-taking abilities, and achievement" (pp. 156–157). Working through problems in rough drafts together and discussing ways to make writing clearer and more meaningful lead group members to internalize values and to expand their role-taking ability.

Expanded role-taking ability is central to cognitive growth because it encourages the formation of alternative perspectives on experiences (Flavell, Botkin, Fry, Wright, & Jarvis, 1968; Johnson-Laird, 1983). That is, through interacting with others, sharing points of view and a range of representations of reality, students construct various models related to how the world operates. Participating in group work requires students to apply these models, and, as far as we currently know, the application develops critical-thinking skills. Students become better, more critical readers of their own work, which in turn helps them become better writers (see Hawkins, 1980; Huff & Kline, 1987).

There are other benefits. Students may actually learn more when collaborating than they do when working alone (Crawford & Haaland, 1972; Laughlin & McGlynn, 1967). Huff and Kline (1987) report that "students working together on assignments have more success in completing them, remain motivated longer, build a sense of group purpose that provides additional motivation, tend to continue into other, higher tasks in the same subject area, and view the instructor more and more favorably as learning and success rates improve" (p. 136).

Many students, particularly older ones, may need time to adjust to collaborative learning, and initially they may be reluctant to help one another write. In most circumstances, the largely risk-free environment offered by the workshop quickly reduces their apprehensions, and students perform at the level set by their teacher's expectations.

Three Stages of Social Bonding

There are three distinct stages of development associated with collaborative learning: the bonding stage, the solidarity stage, and the working stage. Some of the procedures discussed above are designed to help students attain the first two stages, and workshop activities themselves will help keep them on task throughout the third.

Bonding is crucial to an effective classroom environment, but it will not occur unless students identify themselves with their particular group and unless they feel they don't have to compete with their group members. During the bonding stage, group members must adjust to the idea that they will be working closely together for the entire term, and they must develop a sense of community.

If you are successful in creating the conditions that lead to bonding, students will be ready for the solidarity stage, in which the group establishes a social network in response to the dominant and subordinate personalities of its members. This stage usually begins to develop after the class has had several opportunities to work on papers, and students should start to experience a growing sense of confidence in their abilities to read and evaluate one another's work. Furthermore, they recognize their strengths and weaknesses relative to their cohorts and make the adjustments necessary for effective feedback during the composing process. For example, it isn't uncommon for one student to have greater L_2 proficiency than her cohorts. Another may have strong organizational or leadership skills. The result is usually a natural division of responsibility, with members sharing equal but different tasks.

Finally, during the working stage, students come to see the group as a true support network that can be trusted to give honest and worthwhile advice that helps them produce better writing. A desirable goal at this point is a group identity so strong that individual success on an assignment is viewed as group success.

One technique we can use to enhance the bonding process during the first stage involves asking group members to complete joint projects, that is, projects that require the participation of all members. Among younger students, such projects can take the form of collaborative stories or poems. Among older students, they can take the form of reports, where students investigate a topic at school or in their community, or of panel presentations, where members research a topic and then share what they learn with the entire class.

A significant difficulty, however, is the tendency of some students to do very little, forcing the more conscientious members to assume the majority of the task. One way to guard against this problem is to divide the assignment into discrete parts and then have each student periodically complete a progress report that he or she turns in. Another difficulty arises when better students in a group feel that their grade on a project is being lowered by the work of the poorer students. Rewarding students for what they do well, rather than punishing them with a low grade for what they don't do well, helps alleviate such distress.

In fact, grading is commonly a serious obstacle to effective bonding and collaboration. Grades are universal and strong motivators, but they generally fail to solidify the social bonds necessary to make collaboration succeed. They are individual motivators more than group motivators. We suggest that students will respond better to a range of affective factors that teachers can use to stimulate bonding, such as positive reinforcement for group activities.

The Problem of Grading Group Participation

Given the importance of group work on improving bilingual students' writing skills, some teachers may feel compelled to grade the level of participation during workshop activities. We've encountered this compulsion in classes we've observed where students received one grade for bringing a rough draft to class, another for commenting on a fellow student's draft, and so forth.

Although the idea of grading group participation (or what some teachers have come to call "the writing process") may at first glance seem to make good sense, we would argue that it is misconceived and counterproductive. The input we want writers to receive from fellow students must achieve a certain quality if it is to be effective. Grading participation, however, forces teachers to attempt to objectify students' efforts, forces them to try to quantify group interactions. It shifts the task focus significantly from having a thoughtful draft to having a draft.

We would suggest that when a workshop and collaborative learning are functioning well, the students' writing will show it. The reverse is also true. It therefore seems reasonable to suggest that the grades we give finished essays reflect group participation better than any separate or intermediate evaluation. They should serve as sufficient indicators of group involvement. In other words, students in effective work groups should be writing better papers than those in ineffective groups.

THE TEACHER'S ROLE
IN A WRITING WORKSHOP

The aim of the classroom workshop isn't simply to give students opportunities to interact with one another, even though this is an important aim. It is also to create more opportunities for teachers to interact with students as the students are writing. The interaction is designed to provide instruction during the composing process, when it is most beneficial.

If you have managed to keep some space between work groups, you will be able to circulate among them as they work. As you move about, listen to students discuss their papers. When you can offer suggestions to clarify a point, do so. You will also want to look over as many papers as possible, offering advice on ways to improve them. Your comments will cover a range of issues, from organization to spelling, but occasionally you will see several students with similar problems. In this case, you should get the class' attention and give a short lesson (say 5 or 10 minutes, at the most) for everyone's benefit.

When you offer comments on papers, you are modeling reading as well as writing. That is, you are essentially showing students how they should read one another's papers. You can therefore profitably direct your comments to the student reading a paper rather than to the writer. Be assured that the writer will be paying close attention to what you say. In fact, his or her attention may actually be greater in this case because you are telling a groupmate how to go about assessing the paper.

To be successful at reading student papers in class this way, you have to develop the ability to read quickly. Just as important, you must be able to make fast evaluations and to give concise, positive advice that will help students improve their writing. It's usually wise to begin with praise; even the worst paper usually has something worthwhile in it. Try to make students feel good about themselves as writers while simultaneously offering a realistic evaluation. Then point out *at most* two problems (you don't want to overwhelm children with things to repair), giving concrete suggestions on how to fix them. Don't just say, "This needs more work" or "This isn't clear."

Another beneficial way to interact with students is to conduct short conferences, either individually or in groups of two or three. When conferring, your goal should be to get students to articulate their intentions, how they hope to realize them, and what writing techniques they are using. Let students talk about their papers. When they have finished, read through them to see how well they match what the students say they are trying to do. Expect some gaps and concentrate on reducing the significant ones.

It is very important that students do most of the talking during a conference. When they explain a composition, they have a wonderful opportunity to practice their oral skills. In addition, describing what they intend to do with the paper reinforces such discourse features as organization, examples, audience, and tone, as we saw in Chapter 5 when explaining the "talk/write" model. We suggest you follow this principle: Our job is not to put language into the head of a child—our job is to get it out. Moreover, many writing specialists believe that when teachers talk rather than listen during a conference, they unconsciously begin to appropriate the text.

Again, with the aim of avoiding overwhelming students with negative feedback, don't tackle more than two points at a time. Furthermore, bilingual students are not likely to show marked, short-term improvement in the subskills areas of spelling, punctuation, and sentence structure, so focus on rhetorical issues related to the text's overall effectiveness. Work on these until the student shows some improvement, but don't dwell on them to such an extent that the student grows bored.

If students are going to do most of the talking in a conference, they will need frequent prompts to keep their minds active. Using questions that guide students to discover for themselves the strengths and weaknesses of a composition is a highly effective strategy (see I. Clark, 1986). For example, if a paper lacks an easily identifiable thesis, you can ask the writer to tell you what claim he or she is making in the paper. Listen carefully and then ask the student to show you where the claim appears in the text. The difficulty will be obvious, and the student will recognize that a crucial part of the paper is lacking. After he or she has articulated the thesis, you can more easily point out where it should appear in the text.

Using an approach in conferences that emphasize questions rather than statements has the advantage of prompting students to think for themselves about what they are doing. It engages them in the processes of critical inquiry and problem solving that are essential to continued improvement in writing performance, because they are discovering things about their writing for themselves. As a result, the revisions they make are their revisions, not the teacher's. This approach involves students in learning by doing, which is the best kind of learning.

MIXED CLASSES: MAINSTREAM AND BILINGUAL STUDENTS

The demographics of your school will determine whether your classes are mixed with both native and nonnative English speakers. If your classes are heterogeneous, there are several important issues you will need to consider as you begin structuring your classroom.

For example, you should be sensitive to the fact that nonnative English speakers may feel inferior to the native English speakers in the class. They may feel as though they have to compete with the mainstream students, which will fuel their anxiety over success.

Bilingual students' fear of failure can seriously handicap your efforts. In a mixed class, this fear is likely to be especially acute because of the presence of native English-speaking peers, whom the bilinguals may believe will ridicule their use of English. Where the fear of failure is strong and where the potential for ridicule is great, students simply withdraw into themselves and refuse to participate in activities (Harter, 1981). Dulay, Burt, and Krashen (1982) argue that fear of failure and subsequent rejection will prevent second-language learners from interacting with native speakers of that second language (also see Rose, 1984).

The classroom workshop can help reduce the anxieties associated with reading and writing. Our discussion of language acquisition in Chapter 3 provides a framework for the dynamics that exist in mixed work groups: They provide a social dimension to school language use that is often missing in other approaches to writing instruction. In fact, we would argue that the collaborative environment of the workshop classroom is central to developing both oral proficiency and academic literacy. Work groups offer opportunities to make meaningful connections with others who are willing to interact in speech as well as writing. They become communities of readers, writers, speakers, and listeners. As the teacher interacts with these communities, she serves as a model for language behavior (specifically Standard English), showing students how to use the four language modes appropriately.

If we accept Edelsky's (1986) conclusion that most of the interference problems bilingual writers have are developmental, mixed classes become excellent places for bilinguals to experiment with language in ways that close developmental gaps. Multiple drafting and revision activities in the classroom workshop result in a significantly risk-free environment. The inevitable mistakes our bilingual students will make during the writing process should not only be allowed but encouraged, because they are an important part of learning. The goal is to ask students to stretch themselves beyond what they think they can do, let them stumble, and then encourage them to go on, to try again. As students work together and share their drafts, it soon becomes clear that the act of writing presents problems that transcend language. The central issue in writing is making meaning, which is fundamentally difficult. Working in a native language rather than a second doesn't eliminate the difficulty, it simply shifts it to a different level.

If we can get our bilingual students to take more risks with English, they will expand their range of skills, which in turn will lead to greater success and to increased confidence in their writing ability (see Kantor, 1985). Confidence and success are crucial to their academic achievement. As Diaz (1986) tell us: "The development of confidence in writing that can accompany the use of process techniques brings . . . a powerful and important by-product for ESL students in learning to write in English" (p. 173).

SAMPLE CLASSROOM ACTIVITIES

Generally, our students' oral language skills will develop in advance of their written language skills, which suggests that you should consider creating writing activities that involve speaking and listening. You need not limit yourself, however, to the "talk/write" model that we have already described. For example, videotape machines can be very useful in combining listening, speaking, and writing activities. You can bring to class tapes of television shows to share with students. Ideally, the show should be only 30 minutes long. Let students watch for several minutes, then turn the sound off so they see the picture without any of the accompanying dialogue. When about 10 minutes of the program is left on the tape, turn off the video machine. Your first writing assignment would ask students to create the missing dialogue. They should complete the assignment cooperatively, which will give them opportunities to read their work aloud. You may even want to try staging a competition for the most inventive dialogue, the most dramatic, the most humorous, the most realistic, and so forth.

After the first task is complete, you should replay the tape with the sound on to let students compare what they wrote with the original. You may want to replay it in short segments, asking students to copy down what they hear, because taking dictation can improve students' mastery of sound-to-symbol correspondences. You can move about the room to assess how well students are doing, carefully pronouncing words or phrases that students have missed.

You can generate another activity on the basis of the student dialogues by asking the class to analyze how their versions differed from the original. With older students, you might ask how their own experiences and backgrounds influenced their perception of the story and the characters. Along similar lines, you might ask students to write an ending for the story, with an explanation of why they think it would turn out as they expect. Playing the remainder of the videotape allows students to compare their endings with the original and is likely to lead to some interesting discussions.

Stories, essays, poems, and newspapers provide similar sources of writing activities. You can read a portion of a text to the class and use it for a variety of writing tasks, from letters to the editor to poems. You can also ask students to bring in their own texts to share with the class or to use for a writing assignment. Community newspapers written in a home language or even letters from friends or relatives outside the United States can prove very interesting to other students, because they contain information not readily available from other sources.

CONCLUSION

We recognize it isn't easy to consider using a workshop method for teaching writing to bilingual students. The traditional approach of drills and exercises seems much more straightforward and would appear to be much more effective. As it turns out, however, this is not the case. What we currently know about language acquisition and writing performance suggests that the workshop approach most closely matches not only the way people produce texts but also the way writing proficiency develops. Moreover, research is beginning to clarify why the errors we see in bilingual writing cannot be remedied through traditional methods, just as it is beginning to show why they can be dealt with developmentally if we treat them as a normal part of language/literacy acquisition.

In our view, writing instruction should be guided by the notion that language is a social action. When it is, we will find a classroom environment that emphasizes frequent writing opportunities as well as meaningful input from peers and teacher. We will find a meaningful context for writing, in that tasks are related to students' experiences. We will also find a workshop methodology that stresses multiple revisions of a paper before it is turned in for evaluation. Likewise, we will find an emphasis on collaborative learning and activities that combine reading, writing, listening, and speaking. Finally, we will find a significant de-emphasis on grammar and mechanics, with a corresponding reduction in error correction.

CHAPTER 9

Who Is Teaching Literacy in Bilingual Programs?

OVERVIEW

Providing an appropriate language program to students who possess a variety of proficiencies and skills in two languages is by no means an easy task. Even under the best of circumstances, when the academic goals of the program are clear and everyone agrees with them, when the teacher is credentialed, experienced, bilingual, and biliterate, there are numerous technical problems that can hinder effective instruction. For example, questions of time and extent of language use in the classroom force teachers to consider how much time should be allotted for each language. Should they be used equally?

When teachers are not bilingual and biliterate, schools normally hire aides who function as interpreters. In such cases, who is ultimately responsible for teaching in the students' native language? How will paraprofessionals be utilized, and how are the roles of teachers and paraprofessionals to be defined?

This chapter addresses these important questions and offers possible alternatives for classroom management and use of the paraprofessional in a bilingual program. In some school districts, there are extreme hardship situations where no bilingual personnel are available, even though many students may be LEP. This chapter examines how to teach in two languages under such conditions.

CLASSROOM MANAGEMENT AND BILINGUAL INSTRUCTION

Managing class time effectively is difficult even when only one language is used. Commonly, curriculum guidelines require too many subjects to be taught in too little time. At the elementary level, for example, teachers must often integrate subject areas, not only for pedagogical reasons but for efficiency. Effective time management becomes even more critical when two languages are used in the classroom, because time allotted for each language constitutes an additional decision teachers have to make.

As a result, teachers are pressured by time constraints into making language-of-instruction decisions that can significantly affect instruction. If one language is preferred over the other, the consequence will often be both affective problems and academic achievement problems that become difficult to reverse. For example, preference for English over the students' native language may produce a sense of unimportance for the minority-language students, leading to a loss in self-esteem and a poor self-concept. Yet preference for the native language will exclude the monolingual English students from instruction. Overusing two languages in the same context when one may suffice can result in not having enough time for all subjects and in neglecting important instruction in content areas. This will ultimately delay students' academic progress.

Alternatives for Language Use

At the elementary level, the typical bilingual classroom will have about 30 students, some of whom are monolingual in English, some of whom are monolingual in a language other than English, and some of whom may be bilingual or LEP. The exact ratios will vary from class to class and from school to school. It is also possible that all students in the classroom may be monolingual in a language other than the language of instruction, such as in second-language immersion programs. We will not address that possibility here because it calls for an instructional approach addressed elsewhere, as in the St. Lambert experiment in Canada (Swain & Lapkin, 1982).

When the student population in the classroom is mixed, there are various alternatives available for using the two languages. One possibility is that teachers will address their classes as a whole using one language. Although there are times when this would be appropriate, in most cases this choice would mean that one of the two groups of students will be ignored. The issue of equity will enter the picture if the same groups of students are consistently being left out of the instructional program.

In order to be equitable, sometimes teachers choose to always use both languages concurrently, that is, they say something in one language and then immediately repeat it in the other language. Although this approach can be appropriate in certain situations, it is important to keep in mind that saying the same thing in two languages takes twice as long. Children of either language will tune out the language they do not know and will listen only to their native language (see Krashen & Biber, 1988). While they are waiting for each language to begin and end, some children may lose interest in the lesson. Thus repeating the same thing in two languages merely to be equitable does not do justice to the concept of equity.

It is important to note that equity in this context should be viewed as something more than simply the equal use of two languages for instruction. In our analysis, equity means that minority-language students receive appropriate instruction that will lead to academic success. It can be achieved by teachers using the students' native language to explain difficult content area concepts or by teachers using English, as long as learning occurs.

The language or languages teachers will choose to use in the various classroom situations will not only condition learning, but will also subtly determine the tone of multicultural tolerance and cooperation in the classroom. We once heard that some teachers used Spanish only to reprimand students, English to praise them. It's easy to imagine what impact this might have on the atmosphere of the classroom. We suggest that language choice and use depend on both the situation and the particular learning task. To accomplish this in the most efficient and equitable way, we recommend that teachers divide classes into flexible groups based on language proficiency.

Practical Examples: Making the Most of Class Time

Grouping students provides the pedagogical advantages associated with a workshop environment, and it also makes it easier to monitor students. Checking for understanding is easier and more accurate, and students can participate more than they can when they are in a traditional classroom.

Although at the middle school and high school levels teachers will want to establish permanent work groups, at the elementary level it is often advantageous to use flexible grouping. With flexible grouping, teachers will reorganize group memberships according to the particular language activity students are performing.

Let's take a 90-minute reading period to illustrate how grouping can work at the elementary level. Teachers would divide the class for reading into three groups according to language and reading level. Group 1 would consist of non-English speakers who are reading in their native language. With this group, teachers would use the students' native language exclusively. Group 2 would be monolingual English speakers who are reading in English, so teachers would conduct the lesson solely in English. Group 3 would be LEP students literate in their native language who are reading in both English and the native language. Teachers would use the two languages when necessary to make connections and explanations.

The content of the lesson and the language of instruction would be different for each group. Teachers would allot 20–30 minutes to meet with one group before moving on to the next, and so on. When teachers aren't part of a group, the other two may be involved in collaborative tasks, they may be working at independent learning centers, or they may be meeting with paraprofessional aides for a reading comprehension or writing follow-up lesson.

Class structure would differ if teachers used a literature-based method of reading instruction like the Comprehensive Approach. Teachers might begin by addressing the entire class in English, using a literary work or fairy tale the students already know. After reading part of the text and discussing certain aspects of it in English, teachers could divide the class into two groups: the monolingual English group, which would work collaboratively on comprehension questions based on the text without the teacher, and the non-English and limited-English-proficient group, which would continue to work with teachers using the native language and English to discuss main ideas, new English vocabulary, and so forth. If an aide is available, teachers would devote this time to native-language reading for non-English speakers. The LEP group could be subdivided so that part would work in the native language, the other in English with either the teacher or the aide.

Another alternative for the same situation might be the following: Aides might meet first with the monolingual English group to discuss their work. Teachers would meet with the non-English speakers for ESL work. Then the entire class would come together to read from the text for comprehension and interpretation activities in English. Following this, students could regroup for a collaborative writing task, during which teachers and aides would circulate and provide individual assistance to students as needed.

The next day, the non-English speakers use the papers they have written to discuss sentence patterns, vocabulary, and purpose. The next day, teachers would meet with the monolingual English students for a writing task, while aides would meet with the non-English speakers to discuss and continue their writing. The groups vary according to language and task.

Many times teachers will want to address the entire class, such as when discussing routine classroom procedures, when resolving interaction problems among students, or when introducing a new unit of study. A practical rule of thumb for language use is that if the context is clear there is no need to repeat the same thing in two languages. In the case of scarce resources, English may be selected for efficiency. For example, routine situations and established classroom procedures like lining up to go to recess are clear in themselves and require only some modeling. It will suffice to elicit the right response from non-English speakers and will serve to expand the students' receptive language. Lessons in music, art, and physical education, as well as manipulative lessons in math or science can be carried out entirely in English (see Krashen & Biber, 1988). In the latter case, however, some concepts may have to be explained using the students' native language.

During math, for example, if the class is learning a skill but the students speak two different languages, teachers may begin the lesson in the minority language with an introduction of the concept to be learned. This approach will help orient the students who speak no English to what will happen next. While this takes place, monolingual English students can begin correcting math homework from the previous day or can review. Teachers would then proceed with the lesson using English but complementing the lesson with audiovisuals and manipulatives. If the concept is particularly difficult, teachers would review it at the end of the lesson in the minority language, to make sure all students understood it.

Students will be more attentive to instruction delivered in their second language if they know what the context and the purpose of the lesson are than if the lesson is delivered in English and they have no idea what the whole thing is about. The strategy, therefore, is to preview the material before presenting it and then to review it afterwards. A meaningful follow-up to this type of lesson would be a collaborative learning activity, where students have a certain task to accomplish together. A writing activity such as those described in Chapter 8 would be appropriate.

At the secondary level, schoolwide organization can play a more significant role in grouping for language instruction than at the elementary level, where teachers have the flexibility to integrate various subjects using flexible groupings throughout the day. Although secondary school teachers may use two languages and collaborative groupings in the workshop approach within a traditional one-subject/one-period organization, the school may adopt an organization that tracks students by language.

Subjects may be offered in minority languages, and only those students who speak that language may enroll. For example, a school might offer an algebra class open exclusively to Armenian-speaking students and taught in Armenian by an Armenian-proficient teacher. Such programs exist in some junior high schools where there is a large number of newly arrived immigrants.

Along similar lines, but unfortunately not as well intended, some secondary schools offer such subjects as "ESL History" or "ESL Math" for LEP tracks. These classes invariably have a low content level, owing to the attempt to teach both content matter and English at the same time. (In Chapter 6, we discussed the problem inherent in assuming that sheltered English equals ESL.)

The main problem resulting from language tracking is obvious. The minority-language students are immediately segregated by language and ethnicity and never have the opportunity to interact with native English speakers. Although in some cases they may receive academic training and may make some short-term academic progress, their separation from the mainstream is likely to have serious social, cultural, and academic consequences over the long term. Students in ESL content courses face even greater difficulties. Generally, the designation "ESL" indicates that somehow instruction in these classes will be different (and of lesser quality) than what other students receive. The resulting stigma can be permanently damaging.

We believe that a much better solution to the technical question of appropriate language instruction for secondary school students is to provide instruction in both the native language and English. If a bilingual teacher is not available, a modification in teaching strategies using either a bilingual aide or other tutorial assistance would be preferable to schoolwide tracking.

Clearly, it will not be sufficient to use only modified teaching strategies in English. It will be necessary to use students' native language for difficult concepts, to make connections with and provide a cognitive base for English. Bilingual paraprofessionals will have to be assigned for each period as content-area interpreters. Later in this chapter we discuss specific techniques for using bilingual aides. However, at this point it is worth mentioning the potential usefulness available in bilingual peer tutors.

Bilingual Peer Tutors

Bilingual peer tutors are an inexpensive source of assistance rarely used in an official way in junior and senior high schools. Yet they can be an invaluable source of help for the teacher by fulfilling the role of interpreter and assistant. For example, if a sufficient cadre of bilingual peer tutors were recruited school-wide, trained in interpreting techniques, and assigned to each subject period to work for academic credit with a group of LEP students in their native language and in English, immense benefits would be derived for students and teachers alike. The LEP students would have models of bilingualism and scholarship, they would receive assistance in academic areas, and would have emotional support in the form of "buddies." In other words, they would have someone who cared about their academic achievement and who could help them bridge the gaps between mainstream and native culture.

Using bilingual peer tutors has tremendous potential for developing informal peer networks that will have an additional hidden benefit: to keep students in school. Many studies indicate that students who drop out do so because "there was no one who cared." They are those students who have no positive relationships with good students. Most teenagers view school as the place to go to see their friends. A lack of meaningful relationships in school contributes to student dropout (see "National Commission on Secondary Schooling for Hispanics, 1984). The social and personal benefits that peer tutors would derive from this experience will be substantial for them as well and will surpass the school credit they would receive.

Team Teaching

At the elementary level, the reality of classroom demographics is likely to be more complex than we can adequately describe in this text, where we are forced to deal in generalities. For example, teachers may have only two or three students who speak no English at all; the rest of the class may be at various levels of English proficiency and native-language literacy. In such a case, teachers may want to attempt a team-teaching approach with another teacher. For part of the day, the few students who speak no English would go to another teacher who has several students who speak no English, and they would be involved in native-language instruction and ESL lessons as a group. This type of teaming could also be done in secondary schools on a one-to-one basis between teachers of the same subjects.

Team teaching works well, especially at the elementary level, to maximize teachers' expertise and language knowledge. Teachers who are bilingual in the students' native language can do all the native-language instruction while mono-lingual English teachers can do the English-language instruction, taking care that students are not segregated by language for the entire day. Groups of students can travel from one teacher to the other for specific segments of the day. Another possibility is for one teacher to do all language arts instruction while another does all the math and science instruction, thereby minimizing planning time and giving students the benefit of the teacher's subject expertise.

THE BILINGUAL PARAPROFESSIONAL

The approaches we have discussed to this point have emphasized bilingual teachers, even though many who work with language-minority students are English monolingual. In fact, more often than not, the teacher assigned to a bilingual classroom is monolingual and must rely on the assistance of a bilingual aide. Even when teachers are bilingual, as we saw, it is necessary to exercise much care and skill to use the two languages appropriately. The situation is further complicated when teachers must use paraprofessionals as interpreters.

Research on the role of the bilingual aide indicates that, when properly used, aides can make a significant difference in the classroom. Teachers' jobs become more manageable, and they themselves become more productive be-cause they have more opportunities for individualized instruction. In addition, the research suggests that aides often serve as cultural links with the community, fulfilling students' need to identify with people within that community (Godwin, 1977; La Fontaine, 1971; C. Perez, 1971; S. Perez, 1979; Zalk, 1975).

Little research, however, deals specifically with how bilingual aides can best be used in the classroom, which has led to some confusion regarding their role and associated teacher expectations. Some teachers reportedly underemploy their aides, giving them either menial tasks or none at all. Others give them too much responsibility (McIlhenny, 1979). Furthermore, research dealing with competencies and training of bilingual aides indicates that they are unprepared to perform in the very areas for which they are employed (Mesa Community College, 1976; Seymann, 1979). Because existing research offers no specific guidelines on the use of bilingual aides, it often will be up to individual teachers to develop a relationship with the bilingual aide that will ultimately benefit students. Some districts and schools support this process by providing guidelines established specifically for students in the community.

Because aides are not trained as instructors, teachers have to provide both guidance and monitoring for the relationship to work. Teachers generally have to train aides both to act as interpreter and to teach, because subjects like reading will have to be taught primarily in the students' native language. Teachers therefore assume an additional responsibility: training and monitoring aides.

If a teacher were to ask the aide to provide native-language instruction without giving any directions or guidance or without overseeing the nature of the aide's interaction with the class, students might feel that they were not good enough for the teacher, that the teacher had abandoned them. The teacher would not be able to assess students' progress. Moreover, students would face the prospect of suffering academically because they are taught by a person without proper training.

Issues of Power and Authority

When aides are used inappropriately, additional difficulties arise that can impair learning. If teachers assume responsibility for mainstream students and aides responsibility for language-minority students, the result is a separation of power. Aides will elicit a greater response from students than teachers by virtue of being, in most cases, from the same ethnic and cultural background as the students and by virtue of speaking their language. Students may identify with and relate to aides to the point that they will not cooperate with their teachers. Classes become divided: A lower status is subtly assigned to students taught by aides, while a higher status is assigned to those taught by teachers. The result is what has been referred to as a "hidden curriculum" (Apple, 1982), in which students learn to assume a lower role in the classroom, a role that will be acted out in lives outside school.

Given the potential for division in this sort of environment, it isn't surprising to find the teacher's authority questioned by mainstream and language-minority students alike. We aren't using "authority" in any controlling sense, of course. We aren't implicitly advocating a teacher-centered classroom. In using "authority," we are describing a teacher's accountability for student learning and student safety, and we are describing the teacher's role in eliciting cooperation and respect from all students. If students refuse to cooperate with a teacher and only respond to an aide, the relationship between teacher and students is broken. No possibility for dialogue will exist, and any learning initiated by the teacher will be difficult. The position of the teacher will be weakened for all students.

To avoid these problems, teachers will have to actively monitor native-language instruction by providing aides with long-range as well as daily lesson plans. We can use reading instruction as an example that will illustrate how to use these plans. It will be much easier if teachers use the same texts for native-language reading as for English reading. They will be familiar with the content, won't have to engage in additional preparation, and will be able to provide their aides with at least a list of comprehension questions to ask students.

As we mentioned in Chapter 6, teachers will want to think about the availability of texts in both English and the students' native language when selecting materials. Aides can be a valuable resource at this point, and asking them to help with selections can form a useful bond. Some languages, such as Spanish, have an abundance of reading materials. For a third-grade class, for example, teachers could select *Ramona the Pest* in English and have *Ramona La Chinche* available in Spanish for Spanish reading instruction directed by the aide. When planning lessons in English, teachers should provide copies to aides, asking them to translate the materials into Spanish. Most of the activities, such as critical thinking, problem solving, comprehension questions, and writing tasks, teachers will do in English with a group of monolingual English-speaking students, aides can do in Spanish with a group of monolingual Spanish-speaking students. By ensuring that aides have a copy of the lesson plan, teachers will be able to monitor closely the aide's instruction in the students' native language.

The Aide as Interpreter

Although we don't define bilingual aides as professional interpreters, the set of principles that professionals use can be very beneficial to teachers and aides alike. One of the more common interpreter training principles from the Monterey Language Institute, for example, is the view of the interpreter as a mirror of the person whose speech is being translated. Interpreters do not edit or personalize the text; they translate it in the other language, taking care that the *exact message* is getting across. This process generally requires training and skills that para-professionals do not necessarily have. Although some research has addressed competency issues of classroom aides, none exists that explores specifically the role of the aide as interpreter in the bilingual classroom. The discussion that follows therefore is based on our own experience as interpreters and as bilingual teachers.

The translation process involves many skills. For example, interpreters must remember what a person has said, then select the correct words that render that particular meaning. The person for whom they are translating must express thoughts very clearly so interpreters will not have any doubts as to what a particular statement actually meant. The more ambiguous the original statement, the more uncertain the translation will be. Thus teachers who are using aides as interpreters must also have skills that will facilitate the process. They must speak clearly and unambiguously. They must keep the passages to be translated short to help aides remember what to translate.

If we apply these principles to the classroom situation, we see that the role of the bilingual aide as interpreter should be that of the teacher's voice. The aide's body language should reflect the general tone of the teacher's statement. If the teacher is stating something serious, the aide should not smile while translating. If the teacher's tone of voice is firm, so should be the aide's. Standing side by side during a translation for the whole class can facilitate such modeling.

Checking for accuracy is something teachers will have to address. Some indications that aides may not be translating accurately are inappropriate student responses, such as laughter following a serious statement, puzzled looks on the students' faces, or restlessness.

Teachers must also be aware of the time that exists between their statements and the translation. If a teacher says one sentence in English and the aide translates it into five sentences, no doubt elaborating at some length, students are likely to lose interest.

We would suggest that teacher authority is defined in the translation process. Consider a situation in which a teacher says to an aide, without looking at students: "Tell them to get ready to go to recess." Then, without waiting for the aide to translate, the teacher walks away to do something or attend to someone. The aide will then stand in front of the class, alone, giving the direction to students directly in their native language. Students will follow the aide's direction and may begin to identify with him or her. Thus the teacher has become separated from the students by giving the appearance of not caring whether they follow directions. Teacher authority is weakened. A division of power similar to what we discussed earlier is linked to a seemingly simple translation process.

As a desirable alternative, we would suggest a situation in which teachers and aides stand side by side before the students. The teacher says to the class in English: "Please get ready to go to recess." The aide translates while the teacher remains unmoving, watching students to see that they follow the direction. Using a smile or direct comments, the teacher praises students who comply with the direction. The teacher maintains authority and is clearly assuming responsibility for the class, regardless of being monolingual.

Given that they are involved in teaching, aides often have to make decisions that professional interpreters don't. For example, when it is not necessary to translate everything verbatim, to save time a teacher may want only key concepts translated. In this case, the aide will have to do some editing. The important point here is that the teacher selects what should and should not be translated and does not leave the decision entirely to the aide to make on the spot, without any idea of what the teacher's goal in the lesson might be. Teachers must thus let aides know in advance what the key concepts of the lesson are and how translations are to occur. If a preview-review approach is being used, teachers will have to meet with aides before class to explain what the lesson will be about and what should be said to students so the message is clearly delivered.

The importance of communication between teachers and aides cannot be underestimated. We once observed a situation where a monolingual teacher gave a long introduction to a lesson, in English, not noticing that his aide was busy with some paperwork at the other end of the room. After speaking for about 10 minutes, the teacher turned to the aide and said: "Tell them what I said." Of course, the aide couldn't. He had not even been listening to the teacher at all! Needless to say, that was not one of the better lessons we ever observed.

In giving a general introduction to a lesson for the whole class, it would be best if one or the other language were used, such as we described earlier in preview-review. If it seems imperative that a long explanation needs to be translated, the teacher should summarize the main points at the end and ask the aide to translate only those. This will ensure accuracy and integrity in the meaning of the lesson.

Hardship Cases: Managing without an Aide

In some cases, aides who speak students' native language may not be available, either because of lack of money to hire them or because there is no one in the community who speaks that language other than the children's parents, who may themselves be monolingual. All possibilities should be exhausted before giving up on the goal of using the native language.

Although the difficulties are great and the educational objectives limited, adults who are monolingual in the students' native language *can* be of help. Serving as volunteers, they can read to the students in the native language, listen to them read, help them write, and can help them with content-area materials like math. Teachers will have to set up a procedure that will not require constant communication with the volunteer. Enlisting such native language help is important for both academic and affective reasons. It makes a clear statement: the teacher values the students' language and culture. Students will recognize they have entered a positive environment, where they are accepted for what they are. They will feel infinitely more secure when they have to deal with context in a foreign language.

Managing without Materials

Availability of materials in the native language for LEP students is also a problem for certain languages. Teachers may have to write to the various consulates to ask how to obtain children's books and dictionaries in those languages. Sometimes materials can be obtained free of charge through international benevolent societies. Materials in languages such as Spanish are available everywhere, and often even poorer districts will have some state, federal, or other funds for bilingual programs.

Instructional methodology will have to be drastically modified to teach content material to students who speak no English. Many of the techniques we discussed within our Comprehensive Approach can be modified to account for lack of instruction in native language. For example, each LEP student can be paired with a monolingual English buddy who has the task of assisting that child. Collaborative groups can be formed to facilitate the integration of LEP students, with one or two LEP children in each group. In short, teachers must ensure that the non-English-speaking students succeed academically by creating an ambience where the instructional content is free of undue anxiety and is contextually clear.

CONCLUSION

In this chapter we discussed organizational and technical issues that facilitate or hinder the success of a language program. Two issues of major concern are language use in the classroom in terms of time allotment, and situations and use of the bilingual paraprofessional when the teacher does not speak the language of the students.

We examined classroom management and offered suggestions for grouping students for directed instruction and collaborative learning to maximize use of time and language in the appropriate situations. We applied some of the principles used by professional interpreters to analyze the role that the translation process has in defining teacher's and aide's authority in the classroom. This area has not been fully explored by research and certainly merits further attention.

Finally, we offered suggestions for providing as meaningful a language program as possible to LEP students in hardship cases, realizing that such suggestions cannot fully substitute for the use of the students' native language. We recommend that teachers actively seek out native-language assistance from the community in the form of volunteers who might even be monolingual in the students' native language. This procedure will give a higher stature to the minority language and a sense of greater worth to the language-minority students.

Dual-language instruction is one of the more challenging tasks that a teacher can take on. But we believe that it is also one of the more rewarding. Our goal throughout this text has been to argue for more and better instruction at all grade levels, and we have explicitly called for less concern with functional oral proficiency and greater concern for literacy. This interest in literacy extends beyond our desire to help teachers improve their students' academic performance. It is linked to what often seems an old-fashioned notion: that the ability to read and write well can help children's minds soar into the limitless realm of human potential.

References

Abbott, V., Black, J., & Smith, E. (1985). The representation of scripts in memory. *Journal of Memory and Language, 24*, 179–199.

Adams, J. A. (1987). A study of the reading process of selected ESL college students. *Dissertation Abstracts International, 49*, 01A. (University Microfilms No. 88–04, 199).

Amastae, J. (1981). The writing needs of Hispanic students. In B. Cronnell (Ed.), *The writing needs of linguistically different students*. Washington, DC: SWRL Educational Research and Development.

Anastasi, A. (1980). Culture-free testing. In G. Lindzey (Ed.), *A history of psychology in autobiography* (Vol. 7). San Francisco: W. H. Freeman.

Anastai, A., & Cordova, F. (1953). Some effects of bilingualism upon the intelligence test performance of Puerto Rican children in New York City. *Journal of Educational Psychology, 44*, 1–19.

Apple, M. (1980). *Reproduction, contestation and curriculum*. (Occasional papers 8). Buffalo: University of New York, Faculty of Educational Studies.

Apple, M. (1982). *Cultural and economic reproduction in education*. London: Routledge and Kegan Paul.

Aronowitz, S., & Giroux, S. (1988). Schooling, culture, and literacy in the age of broken dreams: A review of Bloom and Hirsch. *Harvard Educational Review, 58*, 172–194.

Baddeley, A. D. (1986). *Working memory*. New York: Oxford University Press.

Bailey, R., & Fosheim, R. (Eds.). (1983). *Literacy for life: The demand for reading and writing*. New York: Modern Language Association.

Bates, E. (1976). *Language and context*. New York: Academic Press.

Bates, E. (1979). *The emergence of symbols: Cognition and communication in infancy*. New York: Academic Press.

Bates, E., Camaioni, C., & Volterra, V. (1975). *Communicazione nel primo anno di vita.* Rome: Mulino.

Baugh, J. (1984). *Language in use: Readings in sociolinguistics.* Englewood Cliffs, NJ: Prentice-Hall.

Beach, R., & Liebman-Kleine, J. (1986). The writing/reading relationship: Becoming one's own best reader. In B. Petersen (Ed.), *Convergences: Transactions in reading and writing.* Urbana, IL: National Council of Teachers of English.

Beck, I. L. (1984). Developing comprehension: The impact of the directed reading lesson. In R. Anderson, J. Osborn, & R. Tierney, (Eds.), *Learning to read in American schools.* Hillsdale, NJ: Lawrence Erlbaum.

Bender, T. (1982). *Community and social change in America.* Baltimore: Johns Hopkins University Press.

Bennett, W. (1984). To reclaim a legacy: Text of a report on humanities in higher education. *Chronicle of Higher Education,* November 28, 16–21.

Betancourt, F., & Phinney, M. (1988). Sources of writing block in bilingual writers. *Written Communication, 5,* 461–478.

Bewley, R. K. (1987). The effect of prior knowledge and reader interest on fourth and sixth grade students' reading comprehension. *Dissertation Abstracts International, 49,* 01A. (University Microfilms No. 88–02, 002).

Bilingual Education Act. (1968). *United States Statutes at Large, 81,* 817.

Bizzell, P. (1984). William Perry and liberal education. *College English, 46,* 447–454.

Bizzell, P. (1988). Arguing about literacy, *College English, 50,* 141–153.

Bloom, A. (1987). *The closing of the American mind: How higher education has failed democracy and impoverished the souls of today's students.* New York: Simon & Schuster.

Bloom, L. (1970). *Language development: Form and function in emerging grammars.* Cambridge, MA: MIT Press.

Bloom, L. (1973). *One word at a time: The use of single-word utterances before syntax.* The Hague: Mouton.

Bock, J. K. (1982). Toward a cognitive psychology of syntax: Information processing contributions to formulations. *Psychology Review, 89,* 1–47.

Brooks, N. (1964). *Language and language learning: Theory and practice.* Orlando, FL: Harcourt, Brace, Jovanovich.

Brown, G., & Yule, G. (1983). *Discourse analysis.* Cambridge: Cambridge University Press.

Bruck, M., Lambert, W., & Tucker, G. (1974). Bilingual schooling through the elementary grades: The St. Lambert project at grade seven. *Language Learning, 24,* 183–204.

California State Department of Education. (1981). *Schooling and language minority students: A theoretical framework.* Los Angeles: Evaluation, Dissemination, and Assessment Center.

California State Department of Education. (1984). *Case studies in Bilingual Education.* Sacramento, CA: State Department of Education.

California State Department of Education. (1985). *Model curriculum standards.* Sacramento, CA: State Department of Education.

Calkins, L. (1983). *Lessons from a child.* Exeter, NH: Heinemann.

Campbell, J. (1959). *The masks of God: Primitive mythology.* New York: Viking Press.

Canale, M., & Swain, M. (1980). Theoretical bases of communicative approaches to second language teaching and testing. *Applied Linguistics, 1,* 1–47.

Caplan, R., & Keech, C. (1980). *Showing-writing: A training program to help students be specific.* Berkeley: University of California Press.

Carbo, M. (1978). Teaching reading with talking books. *The Reading Teacher, 32,* 267–273.

Carbo, M. (1987). Deprogramming reading failure: Giving unequal learners an equal chance. *Phi Delta Kappan, 69,* 197–202.

Carnoy, M. (1974). *Education as cultural imperialism.* New York: McKay.

Carroll, J. B. (1986). Second language. In R. F. Dillon & R. J. Sternberg (Eds.), *Cognition and instruction.* San Diego: Academic Press.

Chall, J. (1983). *Learning to read: The great debate,* New York: McGraw-Hill.

Chall, J., Heron, E., & Hilferty, A. (1987). Adult literacy: New and enduring problems. *Phi Delta Kappan, 69,* 190–196.

Chomsky, C. (1976). After decoding: What? *Language Arts, 53,* 288–296.

Christiansen, T., & Livermore, G. (1970). A comparison of Anglo-American and Spanish-American children on the WISC. *Journal of Social Psychology, 81,* 9–14.

Clark, H., & Clark, E. (1977). *Psychology and language.* Orlando, FL: Harcourt, Brace, Jovanovich.

Clark, I. (1986). Perceived literacy in the home and its impact on the writing of college freshmen. Unpublished manuscript: Los Angeles, University of Southern California.

Clark, W. (1968). An evaluation of two techniques of teaching freshmen composition. *Final Report.* Colorado Springs: Air Force Academy.

Colby, B., & Cole, M. (1976). Culture, memory and narrative. In R. Horton & R. Finnigan (Eds.), *Modes of thought.* New York: Academic Press.

Cooper, M. (1986). The ecology of writing. *College English, 48,* 364–375.

Corrigan, R. (1978). Language development as related to stage 6 object permanence development. *Journal of Child Language, 5,* 173–189.

Crawford, J., & Haaland, G. (1972). Predecisional information seeking and subsequent conformity in the social influence process. *Journal of Personality and Social Psychology, 23,* 112–119.

Cummins, J. (1976). The influence of bilingualism on cognitive growth: A synthesis of research findings and explanatory hypothesis. *Working Papers on Bilingualism,* 1–43.

Cummins, J. (1979). Linguistic interdependence and the educational development of bilingual children. *Review of Educational Research, 49,* 222–251.

Cummins, J. (1980). The cross-lingual dimensions of language proficiency: Implications for bilingual education and the optional age issue. *TESOL Quarterly, 2,* 175–187.

Cummins, J. (1981a). The role of primary language development in promoting educational success for language minority students. In California State Department of Education, Office of Bilingual Bicultural Education. *Schooling and language minority students: A theoretical framework.* Los Angeles: California State University, Evaluation, Dissemination and Assessment Center.

Cummins, J. (1981b). Age on arrival and immigrant second language learning in Canada: A reassessment. *Applied Linguistics, 2,* 132–149.

Cummins, J. (1983). *Heritage language education: A literature review.* Toronto: Ministry of Education, Ontario.

Cummins, J. (1988). *Empowering minority students*. Sacramento, CA: California Association for Bilingual Education.

Cummins, J., & Swain, M. (1986). *Bilingualism in education: Aspects of theory, research and practice*. London: Longman.

Daly, J. (1977). The effects of writing apprehension in message encoding. *Journalism Quarterly, 72*, 10–14.

Daly, J., & McCroskey, J. (Eds.). (1984). *Avoiding communication*. Beverly Hills: Sage.

Diaz, D. (1986). The writing process and the ESL writer: Reinforcement from second language research. *The Writing Instructor, 5*, 167–175.

Dillon, G. (1981). *Constructing texts: Elements of a theory of composition and style*. Bloomington: Indiana University Press.

Dobson, L. (1988). *Connections in learning to write and read: A study of children's development through kindergarten and grade one. Technical Report No. 418.* Bolt, Beranek, & Newman. (ERIC Document Reproduction Service No. ED 293 088).

Donelson, K. (1967). Variables distinguishing between effective and ineffective writers in the tenth grade. *Journal of Experimental Education, 35*, 37–41.

Downing, J. (1974). Bilingualism and learning to read. *The Irish Journal of Education, 8*, 77–88.

Dulay, H., Burt, M., & Krashen, S. (1982). *Language two*. New York: Oxford University Press.

Duncan, S., & De Avila, E. (1979). Bilingualism and cognition: Some recent findings. *NABE Journal, 4*, 15–50.

Dunn, L. (1987). *Bilingual Hispanic children on the U.S. mainland: A review of research on their cognitive, linguistic and scholastic development*. Circle Pines, MN: American Guidance Service.

Dyson, A. (1982). The emergence of visible language: The interrelationship between drawing and early writing. *Visible Language, 16*, 360–381.

Dyson, A. (1983). The role of oral language in early writing processes. *Research in the Teaching of English, 17*, 1–30.

Edelsky, C. (1982). Writing in a bilingual program: The relation of L1 and L2 texts. *TESOL Quarterly, 16*, 211–228.

Edelsky, C. (1986). *Writing in a bilingual program: Habia una vez*. Norwood, NJ: Ablex Publishing.

Ehri, L. (1983). A critique of five studies related to letter-name kowledge and learning to read. In L. M. Gentile, M. L. Kamil, & J. S. Blanchard (Eds.), *Reading Research Revisited*. Columbus, OH: Merrill.

Ekstand, L. (1977). *Social and individual frame factors in L2 learning: Comparative aspects*. Papers from the first Nordic Conference on Bilingualism. Helsinki: Helsinfors Universitet.

Epstein, H. (1978). Growth spurts during brain development: Implications for educational policy and practice. In J. Chall & A. Mirsky (Eds.), *Education and the brain* (Vol.2). Chicago: University of Chicago Press.

Ervin, S. M., & Osgood, C. (1954). Language learning and bilingualism *Journal of Abnormal and Social Psychology, 49*, 139–146.

Ervin-Tripp, S. M. (1975). *Language acquisition and communicative choice*. Stanford, CA: Stanford University Press.

Fantini, A. (1982). Emerging styles in child speech: Case study of a bilingual child. In J.

A. Fishman & G. D. Keller (Eds.). *Bilingual education for Hispanic students in the United States*. New York: Teachers' College Press.

Farr, M., & Daniels, H. (1986). *Language diversity and writing instruction*. Urbana, IL: National Council of Teachers of English.

Ferreiro, E., & Teberosky, A. (1982). *Literacy before schooling*. London: Heinemann.

Finnegan, R. (1970). *Oral literature in Africa*. London: Oxford University Press.

Fishman, J. A. (1972). *The sociology of language*. Rowley, MA: Newbury House.

Fishman, J. A. (1976). Bilingual education: What and why? In J. E. Alatis & K. Twaddell (Eds.), *English as a second language in bilingual education*. Washington DC: TESOL

Fishman, J. A. (1981). Language policy: Past, present and future. In C. A. Ferguson & S. B. Heath (Eds.), *Language in the U.S.A.* Cambridge: Cambridge University Press.

Flavell, J., Botkin, P., Fry, C., Wright, J., & Jarvis, P. (1968). *The development of role-taking and communication skills in children*. New York: Wiley.

Flesch, R. (1955). *Why Johnny can't read—and what you can do about it*. New York: Harper & Row.

Flower, L. (1988). The construction of purpose in writing and reading. *College English*, *50*, 528–550.

Flower, L., & Hayes, J. (1981). The pregnant pause: An inquiry into the nature of planning. *Research in the Teaching of English*, *15*, 229–243.

Fodor, J. (1983). *The modularity of mind*. Cambridge, MA: MIT Press.

Fodor, J., Bever, T., & Garrett, M. (1974). *The psychology of language*. New York: McGraw-Hill.

Frege, G. (1977). *Logical investigations*. New Haven: Yale University Press.

Freire, P. (1970). *Pedagogy of the oppressed*. New York: Continuum.

Freire, P., & Macedo, D. (1987). *Literacy: Reading the word and the world*. South Hadley, MA: Bergin & Garvey.

Fries, C. (1962). *Linguistics and reading*. New York: Holt, Rinehart and Winston.

Fritz, M. C. (1987). The culture of the reader, the origin of the text, and how children predict as they read. *Dissertation Abstracts International*, *49*, 01A. (University Microfilms No. 88–03, 043).

Gamby, J. (1983). Talking books and taped books: Materials for instruction, *The Reading Teacher*, *36*, 366–369.

Garcia, E. (1983). *Early childhood bilingualism*. Albuquerque: University of New Mexico Press.

Gardner, R. C. (1980). On the validity of affective variables in second language acquisition: Conceptual, contextual, and statistical considerations. *Language Learning*, *30*, 255–270.

Gardner, R. C. (1983). Learning another language: A true social psychological experiment. *Journal of Language and Social Psychology*, *2*, 219–239.

Garibaldi, A. (1979). Teamwork and feedback: Broadening the base of collaborative writing. Paper presented at the annual meeting of the Conference on College Composition and Communication. (ERIC Document Reproduction Service No. ED 174994).

Genesee, F. (1978). Is there an optimal age for starting second language instruction? *McGill Journal of Education*, *8*, 145–154.

Genesee, F. (1987). *Learning through two languages: Studies of immersion and bilingual education*. Cambridge, MA: Newbury House.

Gibson, E., & Levin, H. (1975). *The psychology of reading*. Cambridge, MA: MIT Press.

Giroux, H. (1983). *Theory and resistance in education: A pedagogy for the opposition*. South Hadley, MA: Bergin & Garvey.

Glass, A., Holyoak, K., & Santa, J. (1979). *Cognition*. Reading, MA: Addison-Wesley.

Godwin, D. (1977). The bilingual teacher aide: Classroom asset. *Elementary School Journal*, 77, 265–267.

Goodlad, J. (1984). *A place called school: Prospects for the future*. New York: McGraw-Hill.

Goodman, K. (1967). Reading: A psycholinguistic guessing game. *Journal of the Reading Specialist*, 6, 126–135.

Goodman, K. (1973). *Miscue analysis*. Urbana, IL: ERIC Clearinghouse on Reading and Communication Skills.

Goody, J. (Ed.). (1968). *Literacy in traditional societies*. Cambridge: Cambridge University Press.

Goody, J. (1972). Literacy and the non-literate. *Times Literary Supplement* (May 12). Reprinted in R. Disch (Ed.), *The future of literacy*. Englewood Cliffs, NJ: Prentice-Hall.

Goody, J., & Watt, I. (1968). The consequences of literacy. In J. Goody (Ed.), *Literacy in traditional societies*. Cambridge: Cambridge University Press.

Graff, H. G. (1987). *The legacies of literacy: Continuities and contradictions in western culture and society*. Bloomington: Indiana University Press.

Graves, D. (1979). Let children show us how to help them write. *Visible Language*, 13, 16–28.

Graves, D. (1981). The growth and development of first grade writers. In D. Graves (Ed.), A case study observing the development of primary children's composing, spelling, and motor behaviors during the writing process. *Final Report*. Durham: University of New Hampshire Press.

Greenfield, P. (1972). Oral or written language: The consequences for cognitive development in Africa, the United States and England. *Language and Speech*, 15, 169–177.

Griswold del Castillo, R. (1984). *La familia: Chicano families in the urban Southwest, 1848 to the present*. Notre Dame, IN: Notre Dame University Press.

Gumperz, J. J. (1982). *Discourse strategies*. Cambridge: Cambridge University Press.

Gunderson, B., & Johnson, D. (1980). Promoting positive attitudes toward learning a foreign language by using cooperative learning groups. *Foreign Language Annuals*, 13, 39–46.

Gundlach, R. (1981). On the nature and development of children's writing. In C. Frederiksen, M. Whiteman, & J. Dominic (Eds.), *Writing: The nature, development, and teaching of written communication*. Hillsdale, NJ: Lawrence Erlbaum.

Gundlach, R. (1982). Children as writers: The beginnings of learning to write. In M. Nystrand (Ed.), *What writers know: The language, process, and structure of written discourse*. New York: Academic Press.

Gundlach, R. (1983). *How children learn to write: Persepctives on children's writing for educators and parents*. Washington, DC: National Institute of Education.

Habermas, J. (1962). *Strukturwandel der Offentlichk: Untersuchungen zu einer kategorie der burgerlichen gesellshaft*. Berlin: Luchterhand.

Hakuta, K. (1984). Bilingual education in the public eye: A case study of New Haven, Connecticut. *NABE Journal*, 9, 53–76.

Hakuta, K. (1986). *Mirror of language*. New York: Basic Books.

Hakuta, K., & Diaz, R. (1984). The relationship between bilingualism and cognitive ability: A critical discussion and some new longitudinal data. In K. Nelson (Ed.), *Children's language* (Vol. 5). Hillsdale, NJ: Lawrence Erlbaum.

Hall, M. (1972). *The language experience approach for the culturally disadvantaged*. Newark, DE: International Reading Association.

Halliday, M. (1979). One child's protolanguage. In M. Bullowa (Ed.), *Before Speech*. Cambridge: Cambridge University Press.

Harder, B. (1984). Cultural attitudes and discourse analysis. *Canadian Journal of Linguistics*, *29*, 115–130.

Hare, V., Rabinowitz, M., & Schieble, K. (1989). Text effects on main idea comprehension. *Reading Research Quarterly*, *24*, 72–88.

Harley, B. (1986). *Age in second language acquisition*. San Diego, California: College Hill Press.

Harste, J., Burke, C., & Woodward V. (1983). *Children's language and world: Initial encounters with print*. (Final Report NIE-G-79-0132). Bloomington, IN: Language Education Departments.

Harter, S. (1981). A model of intrinsic mastery motivation in children: Individual differences and developmental change. In A. Collins (Ed.), *Minnesota Symposium on Child Psychology*, 14. Hillsdale, NJ: Lawrence Erlbaum.

Hatch, E. (1978). *Second language acquisition: A book of readings*. Rowley, MA: Newbury House.

Haugen, E. (1966). *Language conflict and language planning: The case of modern Norwegian*. Cambridge, MA: Harvard University Press.

Hawkins, T. (1980). The relationship between revision and the social dimension of peer tutoring. *College English*, *40*, 64–68.

Heath, S. (1983). *Ways with Words*. Cambridge: Cambridge University Press.

Heath, S. (1986). Literacy and learning in the making of citizens. 1985 Butts Lecture. In *Civic education, pluralism and literacy*. Syracuse, NY: The Center for the Studies of Citizenship and Public Affairs.

Henry, M. K. (1987). Understanding English orthography; Assessment and instruction for decoding and spelling. *Dissertation Abstracts International*, *48*, 11A. (University Microfilms No. 88-00, 951).

Higgs, T., & Clifford, R. (1982). The push toward communication. In T. Higgs (Ed.), *Curriculum, competence and the foreign language teacher*. ACTFL Foreign Language Education Series, 13, Lincolnwood, IL: National Textbooks.

Hillocks, G. (1986). *Research on written composition: New directions for teaching*. Urbana, IL: National Clearinghouse for Research in Education.

Hirsch, E. (1977). *The philosophy of composition*. Chicago: University of Chicago Press.

Hirsch, E. (1987). *Cultural literacy*. Boston: Houghton Mifflin.

Holzman, M. (1986). The social context of literacy education. *College English*, *48*, 27–33.

Holzman, M. (1988). A post-Freirean model for adult literacy education. *College English*, *50*, 177–189.

Hudson, R. (1980). *Sociolinguistics*. Cambridge: Cambridge University Press.

Huff, R., & Kline, C. (1987). *The contemporary writing curriculum: Rehearsing, composing, and valuing*. New York: Teachers College Press.

Hunt, K. (1965). *Grammatical structures written at three grade levels*. NCTE Research Report Number 3. Champaign, IL: National Council of Teachers of English.

Hunter, M. (1970a). *Motivation theory for teachers*. El Segundo, CA: TIP Publications.

Hunter, M. (1970b). *Teach for transfer*. El Segundo, CA: TIP Publications.

Hunter, M. (1980). *Improved instruction*. El Segundo, CA: TIP Publications.

Hymes, D. (1972). On communicative competence. In J. B. Pride & J. Holmes (Eds.), *Sociolinguistics*. Harmonsworth, England: Penguin Books.

Iser, W. (1980). The reading process: A phenomenological approach. In J. P. Tompkins (Ed.), *Reader-response criticism*. Baltimore: Johns Hopkins University Press.

Jackson, N. E., Donaldson, G. W., and Cleland, L. (1988). The structure of precocious reading ability. *Journal of Educational Psychology*, 80, 234–243.

Jacobs, S. (1985). The development of children's writing. *Written Communication*, 2, 414–433.

Jencks, C. (1972). *Inequality: A reassessment of the effect of family and schooling in America*. New York: Basic Books.

Johnson, D. (1980). Group processes: Influences of student-vs-student interaction on school outcomes. In J. McMillan (Ed.), *The social psychology of school learning*. New York: Holt, Rinehart and Winston.

Johnson, D., & Ahlgren, A. (1976). Relationship between students' attitudes about cooperation and competition and attitudes toward schooling. *Journal of Educational Psychology*, 68, 92–102.

Johnson, D., Johnson, R., & Maruyama, G. (1983). Interdependence and interpersonal attraction among heterogeneous and homogeneous individuals: A theoretical formulation and a meta-analysis of the research. *Revew of Educational Research*, 53(1), 5–54.

Johnson, T., & Louis, D. (1985). *Literacy through literature*. Melbourne: Methuen Australia, Ltd.

Johnson-Laird, P. (1983). *Mental models*. Cambridge, MA: Harvard University Press.

Jones, S., & Tetroe, J. (1983). Composing in a second language. In A. Matsuhashi (Ed.), *Writing in Real Time*. Norwood, NJ: Ablex Publishing.

Kantor, K. (1985). Questions, explorations, and discoveries. *English Journal*, 74, 90–92.

Kiechel, W. (1989). The workaholic generation. *Fortune*, 119 (8), 50–62.

Killian, L. (1971). WISC, Illinois test of psycholinguistic abilities and Bender Visual-Motor Gestalt test performance of Spanish-American kindergarten and first grade school children. *Journal of Consulting and Clinical Psychology*, 37, 38–43.

Kintsch, W., & van Dijk, T. (1978). Toward a model of text comprehension and production. *Psychological Review*, 85, 363–394.

Kozol, J. (1985). *Illiterate America*. Garden City, NJ: Anchor Press.

Krashen, S. (1978). On the acquisition of planned discourse: Written English as a second dialect. In M. Douglas (Ed.), *Claremont reading conference: 42nd yearbook*. Claremont, CA: Claremont Graduate School, 173–185.

Krashen, S. (1980). The input hypothesis. In J. Alatis (Ed.), *Current issues in bilingual education*. Washington, DC: Georgetown University Press.

Krashen, S. (1981a). *Second language acquisition and second language learning*. Oxford: Pergamon Press.

Krashen, S. (1981b). The role of input (reading) and instruction in developing writing ability. (Working paper). Los Angeles: University of Southern California.

Krashen, S. (1982). *Principles and practice in second language acquisition*. Elmsford, NY: Pergamon Press.

Krashen, S. (1985). *Writing research, theory, and applications*. Elmsford, NY: Pergamon Press.

Krashen, S., & Biber, D. (1988). *On course: Bilingual education's success in California*. Sacramento: California Association for Bilingual Education.

Krashen, S., & Terrell, T. (1982). *The natural approach: Language acquisition in the classroom*. Oxford: Pergamon Press.

Kroskrity, J. G. (1987). Strategies for language choice in two bilingual preschool classrooms. *Dissertation Abstracts International, 49*, 02A.

La Fontaine, H. (1971). *Para-professionals: Their role in TESOL and bilingual education*. Paper presented at the fifth annual TESOL convention, New Orleans, LA.

Lakoff, G. (1987). *Women, fire, and dangerous things*. Chicago: University of Chicago Press.

Lambert, W. (1977). The effects of bilingualism on the individual: Cognitive and sociocultural consequences. In P. Hornby (Ed.), *Bilingualism: Psychological, social, and educational implications*. New York: Academic Press.

Lambert, W. (1978a). Cognitive and socio-cultural consequences of bilingualism. *Canadian Modern Language Review, 34*, 537–547.

Lambert, W. (1978b). Some cognitive and sociocultural consequences of being bilingual. In J. E. Alatis (Ed.), *International dimensions of bilingual education*. Washington, DC: Georgetown University Press.

Lambert, W. (1983). Additive versus subtractive forms of bilingualism: Confusions regarding programs of immersion. In S. S. Seider (Ed.), *Issues of Language Assessment*. Illinois: State Board of Education.

Lardo, R. 1957, *Linguistics across cultures: Applied linguistics for language teachers*. Ann Arbor: University of Michigan Press.

Lareau, E. (1971). Comparison of two methods of teaching expository composition and evaluation of a testing instrument. *DAI*: 2437–A.

Lassen, N., Ingvar, D., & Skinhoj, E. (1978). Brain function and blood flow. *Scientific American, 10*, 62–71.

Laughlin, P., & McGlynn, R. (1967). Cooperative versus competitive concept attainment as a function of sex and stimulus display. *Journal of Personality and Social Psychology, 7*, 398–402.

Lau versus Nichols (1974). 414 U.S. 563, 94 Supreme Court.

Legaretta-Marcaida, D. (1981). Effective use of the primary language in the classroom. In California State Department of Education. *Schooling and language minority students: A theoretical framework*. Los Angeles: California State University, Evaluation, Dissemination and Assessment Center.

Leibowitz, A. (1976). Language and the law: The exercise of political power through official designation of language. In W. O'Barr (Ed.), *Language and Politics*. Mouton: The Hague.

Leopold, W. (1939–1949). *Speech development of a bilingual child: A linguist's record*, 4 Vols. Evanston, Illinois: Northwestern University Press.

Levelt, W. (1983). Monitoring and self-repair in speech. *Cognition, 14*, 41–104.

Levi-Strauss, C. (1966). *The savage mind*. Trans. Weidenfeld & Nicholson. London: Longman.

Levinson, S. (1983). *Pragmatics*. Cambridge: Cambridge University Press.

Levy-Bruhl, L. (1975). *The notebooks on primitive mentality*. Trans. P. Riviere. New York: Harper & Row.

Luria, A. (1976). *Cognitive development: Its cultural and social foundations*. Trans. M. Lopez-Morrillas & L. Soloturoff. Cambridge, MA: Harvard University Press.

Mackey, W., & Beebe, V. N. (1977). *Bilingual schools for a bicultural community*. Boston, MA: Newbury House.

Macnamara, J. (1972). Cognitive basis of language learning in infants. *Psychological Review*, *79*, 1–13.

MacNamara, J. A. (1966). *Bilingualism and primary education: A study of the Irish experience*. Edinburgh: Edinburgh University Press.

Malt, B. (1985). The role of discourse structure in understanding anaphora. *Journal of Memory and Language*, *24*, 271–289.

Mano, S. (1986). Television: A surprising acquisition source for literacy. *The Writing Instructor*, *5*, 104–111.

Martin, W. (1981). The effects of a program of models-imitation on the writing of seventh grade students. *DAI* 41: 3067–A.

Mason, J. M. (1988). *Reading and writing attempts by kindergarten children after book reading by teachers. Technical Report No. 419*. Bolt, Beranek, & Newman. (ERIC Document Reproduction Service No. ED 293 089).

Mathews, M. (1966). *Teaching to read, historically considered*. Chicago: Chicago University Press.

Matsuhashi, A. (1981). Pausing and planning: The tempo of written discourse production. *Research in the Teaching of English*, *15*, 113–134.

McCrum, R., Cran, W., & MacNeil, R. (1986). *The story of English*. New York: Viking Press.

McLaren, P. (1988). Culture or canon? Critical pedagogy and the politics of literacy. *Harvard Educational Review*, *58*, 211–234.

McLaughlin, B. (1986). Multilingual education: Theory east and west. In B. Spolsky (Ed.), *Language and education in multilingual settings*. San Diego, CA: College Hill Press.

Mesa Community College. (1976). *Research and analysis of competencies needed by the bilingual teacher aide*. Phoenix: Occupational Research Coordinating Unit.

Milan, W. (1982). A generative analysis of the constituent dimensions of bilingual education. In J. A. Fishman and G. D. Keller (Eds.), *Bilingual education for Hispanic students in the United States*. New York: Teachers' College Press.

Miller, J., Chapman, R., Branston, M., & Reichle, J. (1980). Language comprehension in sensorimotor stages V and VI. *Journal of Speech and Hearing Research*, *23*, 284–311.

Modiano, N. (1968). National or mother tongue in beginning reading: A comparative study. *Research in the Teaching of English*, *2*, 32–43.

Moffet, J. (1985). Liberating inner speech. *College Composition and Communication*, *36*, 304–308.

Montgomery County Public Schools. (1976). *End of the school year on the French language immersion program at Four Corners, Maryland.* Baltimore: Maryland County Public Schools.

Naisbitt, J. (1982). *Megatrends: Ten new directions transforming our lives.* New York: Warner Books.

National Commission on Secondary Schooling for Hispanics. (1984). *Make something happen report: Hispanics and urban high school reform.* Washington, DC: Hispanic Policy Development Project.

Nelson, K. (1973). Structure and strategy in learning to talk. *Monographs of the society for Research in Child Development, 38,* (1–2, Serial No. 149).

Ogbu, J. (1983). Minority status and schooling in plural societies. *Comparative Education Review, 2,* 168–190.

Ogbu, J., & Matute-Bianchi, M. (1986). Understanding sociocultural factors: Knowledge, identity and school adjustment. In California State Department of Education, *Schooling and language minority students: A theoretical framework.* Los Angeles: California State University, Evaluation, Dissemination and Assessment Center.

Olson, D. (1977) From utterance to text: The bias of language in speech and writing. *Harvard Educational Review, 47,* 257–281.

Olson, D. (1987). Development of the metalanguage of literacy, *Interchange, 18,* 136–146.

Omaggio, A. (1986). *Teaching language in context: Proficiency oriented instruction.* Boston: Heinle & Heinle Publishers.

Ong, W. (1978). Literacy and orality in our time. *ADE Bulletin, 58,* 1–7.

Ong, W. (1982). *Orality and literacy: The terminologizing of the word.* London: Metheum.

Padilla, A., & Liebman, E. (1982). Language acquisition in the bilingual child. In J. A. Fishman and G. D. Keller (Eds.), *Bilingual education for Hispanic students in the United States.* New York: Teachers' College Press.

Peal, E., & Lambert, W. (1962). The relation of bilingualism to intelligence. *Psychological Monographs: General and Applied, 76,* 1–23.

Perez, C. (1971). *Auxiliary personnel in bilingual education.* Paper presented at the TESOL Convention, New Orleans, March 7.

Perez, S. (1979). How to effectively teach Spanish speaking children, even if you're not bilingual. *Language Arts, 56,* 159–162.

Perfetti, C., & Curtis, M. (1986). Reading. In R. F. Dillon & R. J. Sternberg (Eds.). *Cognition and instruction.* San Diego: Academic Press.

Perl, S., & Wilson, N. (1986). *Through teachers eyes: Portraits of writing teachers at work.* New York: Heineman.

Perry, M. (1980). A study of the effects of a literary models approach to composition on writing and reading achievement. *DAI,* 40:6137–A.

Peterson, P. (1988). Teachers' and students' cognitional knowledge for classroom teaching and learning. *Educational Researcher, 17,* 5–14.

Philips, L. M. (1988). Young readers' inference strategies in reading comprehension. *Cognition and Instruction, 5,* 193–222.

Phillipson, R., & Skutnabb-Kangas, T. (1986). *Linguicism rules in education.* Unpublished doctoral dissertation, Roskilded University, Denmark.

Piaget, J. (1953). *The origins of intelligence in the child*. London: Routledge & Kegan Paul.

Piaget, J. (1955). *The child's construction of reality*. London: Routledge & Kegan Paul.

Piaget, J. (1962). *Plays, dreams, and imitation in childhood*. New York: Norton.

Piaget, J. (1974). *The language and thought of the child*. New York: New American Library.

Pinkham, R. (1969). The effect on the written expression of fifth grade pupils of a series lessons emphasizing the characteristics of good writing as exemplified in selected works from the area of children's literature. *DA* 29: 2613–A.

Quine, W. (1960). *Word and object*. Cambridge, MA: Harvard University Press.

Raimes, A. (1985). What unskilled ESL students do as they write: A classroom study of composing. *TESOL Quarterly, 19*, 229–258.

Raimes, A. (1986). Teaching ESL writing: Fitting what we do to what we know. *The Writing Instructor, 5*, 153–166.

Ramirez, M., & Castaneda, A. (1974). *Cultural democracy, bicognitive development and education*. New York: Academic Press.

Rashotte, C., & Torgesen, J. (1985). Repeated reading and reading fluency in learning disabled children. *Reading Research Quarterly, 20*, 180–188.

Ravitch, D., & Finn, C. (1988). *What do our 17-year-olds know?* New York: Harper & Row.

Reedy, J. (1966). A comparative study of two methods of teaching the organization of expository writing to ninth grade pupils. *DA* 26: 5923–A.

Rehbein, J. (1984). *Diskurs und verstehen: Zur role der muttersprache bei der Textvererbeitung in der Zweitsprache*. University of Hamburg. Reviewed in McLaughlin, 1986.

Reither, J. (1985). Writing and knowing: Toward redefining the writing process. *College English, 47*, 620–628.

Reitsma, P. (1988). Reading practice for beginners: Effects of guided reading, reading-while-listening, and independent reading with computer-based speech feedback. *Reading Research Quarterly, 23*, 219–235.

Restak, R. (1988). *The mind*. New York: Bantam Books.

Rice, M., & Kemper, S. (1984). *Child language and cognition*. Baltimore: University Park Press.

Rivers, W. 1981, *Teaching foreign-language skills* (2nd ed.). Chicago: University of Chicago Press.

Rockhill, K. (1987). Gender, language, and the politics of literacy. *British Journal of Sociology of Education, 8*, 153–167.

Rodriguez, R. (1982). *Hunger of memory: The education of Richard Rodriguez*. Boston: David Godline.

Rosansky, E. (1981). Future perspectives on research on oral language proficiency assessment. Paper presented at the Inter-America symposium on language proficiency assessment. Richmond, VA: Airlie House.

Rosch, E. (1978). *Principles of categorization*. Hillsdale, NJ: Lawrence Erlbaum.

Rose, M. (1988). Narrowing the mind and page: Remedial writers and cognitive reductionism, *College Composition and Communication, 39*, 267–302.

Rose, M. (1984). *Writer's block: The cognitive dimension*. Carbondale, IL: Southern Illinois University Press.

Samuels, D., & Griffore, R. (1979). The Plattsburgh French language immersion program: Its influence on intelligence and self-esteem. *Language Learning, 29*, 45–52.

Sanchez, N. (1987). Bilingual training can be a barrier to academic achievement for students. *Chronicle of Higher Education*, June 10.

Sanford, A., & Garrod, S. (1981). *Understanding written language*. New York: Wiley.

Scardamalia, M., & Bereiter, C. (1983). The development of evaluative, diagnostic, and remedial capabilities in children's composing. In M. Martlew (Ed.), *The psychology of written language: A developmental approach*. London: Wiley.

Schank, R., & Abelson, R. (1977). *Scripts, plans, goals and understanding*. Hillsdale, NJ: Lawrence Erlbaum.

Schlesinger, I. (1971). The production of utterances and language acquisition. In D. Slobin (Ed.), *The ontogenesis of grammar*. New York: Academic Press.

Schumann, J. (1978). The acculturation model for second language acquisition. In R. C. Gingras (Ed.), *Second language acquisition and foreign language teaching*. Arlington, VA: Center for Applied Linguistics.

Scinto, L. (1986). *Written language and psychological development*. Orlando, FL: Harcourt, Brace, Jovanovich.

Scribner, S., & Cole, M. (1981). *The psychology of literacy*. Cambridge, MA: Harvard University Press.

Self, C. (1986). Reading as a writing strategy: Two case studies. In B. Petersen (Ed.), *Convergences: Transactions in reading and writing*. Urbana, IL: National Council of Teachers of English.

Seymann, M. (1979). *The bilingual teacher aide: Competencies and training*. Austin: Dissemination and Assessment Center for Bilingual Education.

Shankweiler, D., & Crain, S. (1986). Language mechanisms and reading disorder: A modular approach. *Cognition, 10*, 139–168.

Shaughnessy, M. (1977). *Errors and expectations: A guide for the teacher of basic writing*. New York: Oxford University Press.

Shayer, D. (1972). *The teaching of English in schools, 1900–1970*. London: Routledge and Kegan Paul.

Skutnabb-Kangas, T. (1984). *Bilingualism or not: The education of minorities*. Clevedon: Multilingual Matters.

Skutnabb-Kangas, T. (1986). Who wants to change what and why: Conflicting paradigms in minority education research. In B. Spolsky (Ed.), *Language and education in multilingual settings*. San Diego: College Hill Press.

Slobin, D., & Welsh, C. (1973). Elicited imitation as a research tool in developmental psycholinguistics. In C. Ferguson & D. Slobin (Eds.), *Studies of child language development*. New York: Holt, Rinehart and Winston.

Smith, F. (1972). *Understanding reading*. New York: Holt, Rinehart, and Winston.

Smith, F. (1983). *Essays into literacy*. London: Heinemann

Smith, F. (1989). Overselling Literacy. *Phi Delta Kappan, 70*, 352–360.

Smith, M. (1939). Some light on the problem of bilingualism as found from a study of the progress in mastery of English among pre-school children of non-American ancestry in Hawaii. *Genetic Psychology Monographs, 21*, 119–284.

Snipper, G. C. (1985). The implementation and effects of the reclassification criteria on the academic achievement of Hispanic language minority students in Los Angeles. Doctoral dissertation, University of California, Los Angeles.

Sponsler, M. (1971). The effectiveness of literary models in the teaching of written composition. *DAI* 32: 2322–A.

Steinbeck, J. (1939). *Grapes of wrath*. New York: Viking Press.

Stefl, L. (1981). The effect of a guided discovery approach on the descriptive paragraph writing skills of third grade pupils. *DAI* 42: 2493–A.

Suaret-Orotio, M. (1987). Towards a psychosocial understanding of Hispanic adaptation to American schooling. In H. Trueba (Ed.), *Success or failure? Learning and the language minority student*. Cambridge, MA: Newbury House.

Swain, M., & Cummins, J. (1979). Bilingualism, cognitive functioning and education. *Language Teaching and Linguistics: Abstracts*, 4–18.

Thibodeau, A. (1964). Improving composition writing with grammar and organization exercises utilizing differentiated group patterns. *DA* 25: 2388.

Thonis, E. (1983). *The English-Spanish connection*. Northvale, NJ: Santillana Publishing Co.

Toukomaa, P., & Skutnabb-Kangas, T. (1977). *The intensive teaching of the mother tongue to migrant children at preschool age*. Unesco, University of Tampere: Research Report 26.

Trevarthen, C. (1974). Communication and cooperation in early infancy: A description of primary intersubjectivity. In M. Bullowa (Ed.), *Before speech: The beginnings of human communication*. Cambridge: Cambridge University Press.

Trimbur, J. (1987). Beyond cognition: The voices of inner speech. *Rhetoric Review*, *5*, 211–221.

Trites, R. L. (1976). Children with learning difficulties in primary French immersion. *The Canadian Modern Language Review*, *33*, 193–207.

Trudgill, P. (1974). *Sociolinguistics: An Introduction*. New York: Penguin Books.

Ulibarri, D., Spencer, N., & Rivas, G. (1981). Language proficiency and academic achievement: A study of language proficiency tests and their relationship to school ratings as predictors of academic achievement. *NABE Journal*, *3*, 47–80.

Ullmann, J. (1963). *Semantics*. Oxford: Basil Blackwell & Mott.

United States Constitution Public Law 90–247, Section 702. (1968). Federal Register, 201–205. Washington, DC: U.S. Government Printing Office.

United States Department of Health, Education, and Welfare. (1970). *Memorandum 35* CFRI 595.

van Dijk, T. (1980). *Macrostructures*. Hillsdale, NJ: Lawrence Erlbaum.

Vinson, L. (1980). The effects of two prewriting activities upon the overall quality of ninth graders' descriptive paragraphs. *DAI* 41: 927–A.

Vygotsky, L. S. (1962). *Thought and language*. Cambridge, MA: MIT Press.

Vygotsky, L. S. (1978). *Mind in society*. M. Cole, V. John-Steiner, S. Scribner, & E. Souberman (Eds.). Cambridge, MA: Harvard University Press.

Warren, R., & Warren, R. (1970). Auditory illusions and confusions. *Scientific American*, *223*, 30–36.

Watson, R. (1985). Toward a theory of definition. *Journal of Child Language*, *12*, 181–197.

Weber, H. (1968). The study of oral reading errors: A survey of the literature. *Reading Research Quarterly*, *4*, 96–119.

Weinreich, E. (1953). *Language in contact: Findings and problems*. New York: Linguistic Circle of New York.

West, W. (1967). A comparison of a "composition equivalencies" approach and a traditional appraoch to teaching writing. *DA* 27:4178–A.

White, E. (1986). *Teaching and assessing writing*. San Francisco: Jossey-Bass.

Whorf, B. L. (1956). *Language, thought and reality: Selected writings of Benjamin Lee Whorf*. J. B. Carroll (Ed.). Cambridge, MA: MIT Press.

Williams, J. D. (1989). *Preparing to teach writing*. Belmont, CA: Wadsworth.

Williams, J. P. (1979). Reading instruction today, *American Psychologist, 34*, 917–922.

Willig, A. (1985). A meta-analysis of selected studies on the effectiveness of bilingual education. *Review of Educational Research, 55*, 269–317.

Witte, S. (1985). Revising, composing theory, and research design. In S. Freedman (Ed.), *The acquisition of written language: Response and revision*. Norwood, NJ: Ablex Publishers.

Woodward, J., & Phillips, A. (1967). Profile of the poor writer. *Research in the Teaching of English, 1*, 41–53.

Yoshioka, J. G. (1929). A study of bilingualism. *Journal of Genetic Psychology, 36*, 473–479.

Zalk, L. (1975). *The role of the paraprofessional in bilingual education*. Paper presented at the National Conference on Urban Education. Kansas City, Missouri, November 24–27.

Zamel, V. (1983). The composing processes of advanced ESL students: Six case studies, *TESOL Quarterly, 17*, 165–187.

Zoellner, R. (1969). Talk-write: A behavioral pedagogy for composition: *College English, 30*, 267–320.

Index

APR 0 2 '92

4075 7 2/99
12- 5/06 - LL - 12/04